Introduction to Business
75-100

Custom Publication for
University of Windsor

MCGRAW-HILL RYERSON LIMITED

Toronto   Montréal   Boston   Burr Ridge, IL   Dubuque, IA   Madison, WI   New York   San Francisco
St. Louis   Bangkok   Bogotá   Caracas   Kuala Lumpur   Lisbon   London   Madrid   Mexico City   Milan
New Delhi   Santiago   Seoul   Singapore   Sydney   Taipei

Business: A Changing World, Canadian Edition, by O. C. Ferrell, Geoffrey Hirt, Elliott Currie and Rick Bates, ISBN 0-07-089837-5.

Interpersonal Skills in Organizations, Second Edition, by Suzanne de Janasz, Karen Dowd and Beth Schneider, ISBN 0-07-288139-9.

Crafting and Executing Strategy: The Quest for Comptetitive Advantage: Concepts and Cases, Fifteenth Edition, by Arthur Thompson, A. J. Strickland III and John Gamble, ISBN 0-07-296943-1

Richard Ivey School of Businesss

Canadian Entrepreneurship and Small Business Management, Sixth Edition, by Wesley Balderson, ISBN 0-07-088868-X

Harvard Business Publishing

Published by McGraw-Hill, a business unit of the McGraw-Hill Companies, Inc., 1221 Avenue of the Americas, New York, NY, 10020.

Product Development Manager, Learning Solutions: Jason Giles
Learning Solutions Custom Print Specialist: Corinne Mohr

ISBN-10: 0-07-089675-5
ISBN-13: 978-0-07-089675-8

Printed and bound in Canada

Table of Contents

Canadian Entrepreneurship and Small Business Management, **Sixth Edition**
by Wesley Balderson

Appendix B

Personal Career Plan

The tools and techniques used in creating a business plan are just as useful in designing a plan to help sell yourself to potential employers. The outline in this appendix is designed to assist you in writing a personalized plan that will help you achieve your career goals. While this outline follows the same general format found in Appendix A, it has been adapted to be more relevant to career planning. Answering the questions presented in this outline will enable you to:

1. Organize and structure the data and information you collect about job prospects, the overall job market, and your competition.

2. Use this information to better understand your own personal strengths and weaknesses, as well as recognize the opportunities and threats that exist in your career development.

3. Develop goals and objectives that will capitalize on your strengths.

4. Develop a personalized strategy that will give you a competitive advantage.

5. Outline a plan for implementing your personalized strategy.

As you work through the following outline, it is very important that you be honest with yourself. If you do not possess a strength in a given area, it is important to recognize that fact. Similarly, do not overlook your weaknesses. The viability of your SWOT analysis and your strategy depend on how well you have identified all of the relevant issues in an honest manner.

I. **Summary**
If you choose to write a summary, do so after you have written the entire plan. It should provide a brief overview of the strategy for your career. State your career objectives and what means you will use to achieve those objectives.

II. **Situation Analysis**
    A. **The External Environment**
        1. **Competition**
            a) Who are your major competitors? What are their characteristics (number and growth in the number of graduates, skills, target employers)? Competitors to consider include peers at the same university or college or in the same degree field, peers at different

universities or colleges or in different degree fields, and graduates of trade, technical, or community colleges.

b) What are the key strengths and weaknesses of the total pool of potential employees (or recent university or college graduates)?

c) What are other university and college graduates doing in terms of developing skills, networking, showing a willingness to relocate, and promoting themselves to potential employers?

d) What are the current trends in terms of work experience versus getting an advanced degree?

e) Is your competitive set likely to change in the future? If so, how? Who are these new competitors likely to be?

2. **Economic conditions**

a) What are the general economic conditions of the country, region, province, and local area in which you live or in which you want to relocate?

b) Overall, are potential employers optimistic or pessimistic about the economy?

c) What is the overall outlook for major job/career categories? Where do potential employers seem to be placing their recruitment and hiring emphasis?

d) What is the trend in terms of starting salaries for major job/career categories?

3. **Political trends**

a) Have recent elections changed the political landscape so that certain industries or companies are now more or less attractive as potential employers?

4. **Legal and regulatory factors**

a) What changes in international, federal, provincial, or local laws and regulations are being proposed that would affect your job/career prospects?

b) Have recent court decisions made it easier or harder for you to find employment?

c) Have global trade agreements changed in any way that makes certain industries or companies more or less attractive as potential employers?

5. **Changes in technology**

a) What impact has changing technology had on potential employers in terms of their need for employees?

b) What technological changes will affect the way you will have to work and compete for employment in the future?

c) What technological changes will affect the way you market your skills and abilities to potential employers?

d) How do technological advances threaten to make your skills and abilities obsolete?

6. **Cultural trends**

a) How are society's demographics and values changing? What effect will these changes have on your:

(1) Skills and abilities:

(2) Career/lifestyle choices:

(3) Ability to market yourself:

      (4)   Willingness to relocate:

      (5)   Required minimum salary:

  b) What problems or opportunities are being created by changes in the cultural diversity of the labour pool and the requirements of potential employers?

  c) What is the general attitude of society regarding the particular skills, abilities, and talents that you possess and the career/lifestyle choices that you have made?

B. The Employer Environment

  1. Who are your potential employers?

    a) Identifying characteristics: industry, products, size, growth, profitability, hiring practices, union/nonunion, employee needs, etc.

    b) Geographic characteristics: home office, local offices, global sites, expansion, etc.

    c) Organizational culture: mission statement, values, priorities, employee training, etc.

    d) In each organization, who is responsible for recruiting and selecting new employees?

  2. What do your potential employers look for in new employees?

    a) What are the basic or specific skills and abilities that employers are looking for in new employees?

    b) What are the basic or specific needs that are fulfilled by the skills and abilities that you *currently* possess and that other potential employees currently possess?

    c) How well do your skills and abilities (and those of your competitors) currently meet the needs of potential employers?

    d) How are the needs of potential employers expected to change in the future?

  3. What are the recent hiring practices of your potential employers?

    a) How many employees are being hired? What combination of skills and abilities do these new hires possess?

    b) Is the growth or decline in hiring related to the recent expansion or downsizing of markets and/or territories? Changes in technology?

    c) Are there major hiring differences between large and small companies? If so, why?

  4. Where and how do your potential employers recruit new employees?

    a) Where do employers make contact with potential employees?

      (1)   College and university placement offices:

      (2)   Job/career fairs:

      (3)   Co-op and internship programs:

      (4)   Headhunting firms:

      (5)   Unsolicited applications:

      (6)   The Internet:

    b) Do potential employers place a premium on experience or are they willing to hire new graduates without experience?

  5. When do your potential employers recruit new employees?

    a) Does recruiting follow a seasonal pattern or do employers recruit new employees on an ongoing basis?

C.   **Personal Assessment**
   1. **Review of personal goals, objectives, and performance**
      a)   What are your personal goals and objectives in terms of employment, career, lifestyle, geographic preferences, etc.?
      b)   Are your personal goals and objectives consistent with the realities of the labour market? Why or why not?
      c)   Are your personal goals and objectives consistent with recent changes in the external or employer environments? Why or why not?
      d)   How are your current strategies for success working in areas such as course performance, internships, networking, job leads, career development, interviewing skills, etc.?
      e)   How does your current performance compare to that of your peers (competitors)? Are they performing well in terms of course performance, internships, co-op placements, networking, job leads, career development, interviewing skills, etc.?
      f)   If your performance is declining, what is the most likely cause?
      g)   If your performance is improving, what actions can you take to ensure that your performance continues in this direction?
   2. **Inventory of personal skills and resources**
      a)   What do you consider to be your marketable skills? This list should be as comprehensive as possible and include areas such as interpersonal skills, organizational skills, technological skills, communication skills (oral and written), networking/team-building skills, etc.
      b)   Considering the current and future needs of your potential employers, what important skills are you lacking?
      c)   Other than personal skills, what do you consider to be your other career-enhancing resources? This list should be as comprehensive as possible and include areas such as financial resources (to pay for additional training, if necessary), personal contacts or "connections" with individuals who can assist your career development, specific degrees or certificates you hold, and intangible resources (family name, prestige of your educational institution, etc.).
      d)   Considering the current and future needs of your potential employers, what important resources are you lacking?

III.   **SWOT Analysis (your personal strengths and weaknesses and the opportunities and threats that may impact your career)**
   A.   **Personal Strengths**
      1.   Three key strengths
         a)   Strength 1:
         b)   Strength 2:
         c)   Strength 3:
      2.   How do these strengths allow you to meet the needs of your potential employers?
      3.   How do these strengths compare to those of your peers/competitors? Do these strengths give you an advantage relative to your peers/competitors?

B. **Personal Weaknesses**
1. Three key weaknesses
    a) Weakness 1:
    b) Weakness 2:
    c) Weakness 3:
2. How do these weaknesses cause you to fall short of meeting the needs of your potential employers?
3. How do these weaknesses compare to those of your peers/competitors? Do these weaknesses put you at a disadvantage relative to your peers/competitors?

C. **Career Opportunities**
1. Three key career opportunities
    a) Opportunity 1:
    b) Opportunity 2:
    c) Opportunity 3:
2. How are these opportunities related to serving the needs of your potential employers?
3. What actions must be taken to capitalize on these opportunities in the short term? In the long term?

D. **Career Threats**
1. Three key career threats
    a) Threat 1:
    b) Threat 2:
    c) Threat 3:
2. How are these threats related to serving the needs of your potential employers?
3. What actions must be taken to prevent these threats from limiting your capabilities in the short term? In the long term?

E. **The SWOT Matrix**

F. **Matching, Converting, Minimizing, and Avoiding Strategies**
1. How can you match your strengths to your opportunities to better serve the needs of your potential employers?
2. How can you convert your weaknesses into strengths?
3. How can you convert your threats into opportunities?
4. How can you minimize or avoid those weaknesses and threats that cannot be converted successfully?

IV. **Resources**
A. **Financial**
1. Do you have the financial resources necessary to undertake and successfully complete this plan (i.e., preparation/duplication/mailing of a résumé; interviewing costs, including proper attire; etc.)?

B. **Human**
1. Is the industry in which you are interested currently hiring? Are companies in your area currently hiring?

C. **Experience and Expertise**
1. Do you have experience from either part-time or summer employment that could prove useful in your current plan?
2. Do you have the required expertise or skills to qualify for a job in your desired field? If not, do you have the resources to obtain them?

V.   **Strategies**
    A.   **Objective(s)**
        1.   Potential employer A:
            a)   Descriptive characteristics:
            b)   Geographic locations:
            c)   Culture/values/mission:
            d)   Basic employee needs:
            e)   Recruiting/hiring practices:
            f)   Employee training/compensation practices:
            g)   Justification for selection:
        2.   Potential employer B:
            a)   Descriptive characteristics:
            b)   Geographic locations:
            c)   Culture/values/mission:
            d)   Basic employee needs:
            e)   Recruiting/hiring practices:
            f)   Employee training/compensation practices:
            g)   Justification for selection:
    B.   **Strategy(ies) for Using Capabilities and Resources**
        1.   Strategy A (to meet the needs of potential employer A)
            a)   Personal skills, abilities, and resources
                (1)   Description of your skills and abilities:
                (2)   Specific employer needs that your skills/abilities can fulfill:
                (3)   Differentiation relative to peers/competitors (why should *you* be hired?):
                (4)   Additional resources that you have to offer:
                (5)   Needed or expected starting salary:
                (6)   Expected employee benefits:
                (7)   Additional employer-paid training that you require:
                (8)   Willingness to relocate:
                (9)   Geographic areas to target:
                (10)   Corporate divisions or offices to target:
                (11)   Summary of overall strategy:
                (12)   Tactics for standing out among the crowd of potential employees:
                (13)   Point of contact with potential employer:
                (14)   Specific elements
                    (a)   Résumé:
                    (b)   Internships/co-op placements:
                    (c)   Placement offices:
                    (d)   Job fairs:
                    (e)   Personal contacts:
                    (f)   Unsolicited:
                (15)   Specific objectives and budget:
        2.   Strategy B (to meet the needs of potential employer B)
            a)   Personal skills, abilities, and resources
                (1)   Description of your skills and abilities:
                (2)   Specific employer needs that your skills/abilities can fulfill:
                (3)   Differentiation relative to peers/competitors (why should *you* be hired?):

(4)   Additional resources that you have to offer:
(5)   Needed or expected starting salary:
(6)   Expected employee benefits:
(7)   Additional employer-paid training that you require:
(8)   Willingness to relocate:
(9)   Geographic areas to target:
(10) Corporate divisions or offices to target:
(11) Summary of overall strategy:
(12) Tactics for standing out among the crowd of potential employees:
(13) Point of contact with potential employer:
(14) Specific elements
    (a) Résumé:
    (b) Internships/co-op placements:
    (c) Placement offices:
    (d) Job fairs:
    (e) Personal contacts:
    (f) Unsolicited:
(15) Specific objectives and budget:

C. Strategy Summary
1. How does strategy A (B) give you a competitive advantage in serving the needs of potential employer A (B)?
2. Is this competitive advantage sustainable? Why or why not?

VI. Financial Projections and Budgets
A. Do you have a clear idea of your budgetary requirements (e.g., housing, furnishings, clothing, transportation, food, other living expenses)?
B. Will the expected salaries/benefits from potential employers meet these requirements? If not, do you have an alternative plan (i.e., a different job choice, a second job, requesting a higher salary)?

VII. Controls and Evaluation
A. Performance Standards
1. What do you have to offer?
Corrective actions that can be taken if your skills, abilities, and resources do not match the needs of potential employers:
2. Are you worth it?
Corrective actions that can be taken if potential employers do not think your skills/abilities are worth your asking price:
3. Where do you want to go?
Corrective actions that can be taken if potential employers do not offer you a position in a preferred geographic location:
4. How will you stand out among the crowd?
Corrective actions that can be taken if your message is not being heard by potential employers or is not reaching the right people:

B. Monitoring Procedures
1. What types and levels of formal control mechanisms are in place to ensure the proper implementation of your plan?
    a) Are your potential employers hiring?
    b) Do you need additional training/education?
    c) Have you allocated sufficient time to your career development?

  d) Are your investments in career development adequate?
   (1) Training/education:
   (2) Networking/making contacts:
   (3) Wardrobe/clothing:
   (4) Development of interviewing skills:
  e) Have you done your homework on potential employers?
  f) Have you been involved in an internship or co-op program?
  g) Have you attended job/career fairs?
  h) Are you using the resources of your placement centre?
  i) Are you committed to your career development?

C. **Performance Analysis**
 1. Number/quality/potential of all job contacts made:
 2. Number of job/career fairs attended and quality of the job leads generated:
 3. Number of résumés distributed:
  a) Number of potential employers who responded:
  b) Number of negative responses:
 4. Number of personal interviews:
 5. Number/quality of job offers:

Building Teams and Work Groups

Learning Points

How do I:
- Form a team and help it progress through developmental stages?
- Form or join a high-performance work team?
- Ensure that all members of a team contribute equally?
- Handle differences in values and work styles in a team setting?
- Allocate team roles and responsibilities?
- Motivate a team to achieve its objectives?

Jeremy was perplexed. He had been looking forward to the first team project in his new job. He had heard how much his new employer valued teamwork. At his previous job, he hadn't encountered teams. He had done virtually all his work on his own, as an individual contributor. This job was going to be different.

At the outset of the project, the group was given a series of projects on which to work. Over the course of the quarter, the group was supposed to evolve into what the team leader called a high-performance work team. But now, at the project's midpoint, Jeremy felt his group was anything but high-performance. Things had started out great. Right away, Jeremy hit it off with his fellow teammates. While the team was diverse in terms of gender, ethnicity, and function, most members had similar interests and got along well with each other. They had even gotten together socially a couple of times during the quarter. At the beginning, the group was very task oriented. They seemed to communicate well and were able to clarify their objective, determine their topic and research priorities, allocate roles and responsibilities, and set up a planning schedule working backwards from their project due date at the end of the quarter.

After a few initial organizing meetings, the group members were left to work on their own. That's where the problems started occurring. In preparation for an interim project due date, Jeremy and his team had planned a team meeting the day before to combine everyone's work and produce the deliverable that the team leader expected the next day. To his chagrin, Jeremy discovered that only he and one other team member were ready. The others had procrastinated and thought they could "wing it." He was contemplating pulling an all-nighter to make up the others' work. "This project is going nowhere," he thought. "Why didn't I just do everything on my own? I could have done better working on my own. This team stuff isn't all it's cracked up to be."

1. What is the situation Jeremy faces? What are the core issues here?

2. How did this situation develop? What could have been done to achieve a different outcome?

3. How would you feel if you were Jeremy? Has a similar situation happened to you?

4. What would you do if you were Jeremy?

5. What should Jeremy do?

"We are a pack animal. From earliest times we have used the strength of the group to overcome the weakness of the individual. And that applies as much to business as to sport."[1]

Tracey Edwards
(Skippered the First Women's
Crew to Circumnavigate
the Globe)

From the popular NBC reality show *The Apprentice* to most of the *Fortune* 500 and many high-tech start-up firms to competitive sports, teams are an everyday occurrence in our personal and work lives. As the nature of work progresses from individually based work to group settings, understanding teams and how to work in team settings and in work groups has become a crucial interpersonal skill. Not everyone is convinced that teams are more effective than individuals working on their own. But the reality is that many organizations are attempting to set up a team-based structure when tackling particular issues or processes, and the ability to work as a team is one of the most commonly required skills in the work environment.[2]

This chapter covers the basics of teamwork. We define teams and detail their importance in business today. We discuss strategies for forming teams and tips for making teams effective and successful. We also include several exercises at the end of the chapter for you to further enhance your team skills, and list resources available for further exploration.

What Is Teamwork?

A team is a formal work group consisting of people who work together to achieve a common group goal.[3] The word *team* is not synonymous with *group*. A **group** is a collection of people who work together but aren't necessarily working collectively toward the same goal. A **team** is composed of three or more interdependent individuals who are consciously working together to achieve a common objective, such as product development, service delivery, or process improvement. A group becomes a team when members demonstrate a commitment to each other and to the end goal toward which they are working. In a team, there is a higher degree of cohesiveness and accomplishment than in a group.[4]

From earliest times, human beings have used teams or groups to overcome the limitations of individuals. Collections of nomads in search of food and land, kingdoms composed of villagers and their leaders, native settlements, wagon trains and pioneers, the crews of ships—all were formed with the idea that more could be accomplished together than by an individual.[5] Even Adam and Eve decided to band together, as do the quasi-"alliances" on the CBS television show *Survivor*. Aside from gains in sheer horsepower, as in the case of a ship's crew, teams exist because few individuals possess all the knowledge, skills, and abilities needed to accomplish all tasks. Simply put, two heads are often better than one.

Within many professional sports teams, we can find shining examples of teamwork. Michael Jordan, one of the world's greatest basketball players and author of the book, *I Can't Accept Not Trying,* writes, "One thing I believe to the fullest is that if you think and achieve as a team, the individual accolades will take care of themselves. Talent wins games, but teamwork and intelligence win championships." He says he never forgot that he was only one-fifth of the effort at any time.[6] Staying with sports for a moment, consider the differences between a gymnastics team and a football team. In gymnastics, the members of a team may work together, but the ultimate achievement of a team is based on the collective efforts of the individual gymnasts. A winning team has the highest combined score. In football, a great quarterback is nothing without a great wide receiver, tight end, or offensive line that can keep him or her from getting sacked. The football team wins when all members work interdependently toward the same goal—passing and rushing their way toward touchdowns.

Returning to the workplace, it is estimated that between 70 and 82 percent of U.S. companies use the team concept, making teamwork skills one of the most commonly required skills in the work environment.[7] Many businesses are adopting a collaborative management approach that encourages sharing ideas and strategies throughout the organization. This collaboration provides many benefits to the organization as well as to the individuals who make up the teams.[8]

Why Teams?

Teaming is more than a phase or a buzzword. If it didn't work, organizations would abandon this strategy for getting work done. There is much evidence that teams can be effective, especially when tasks are complex and task interdependence is high. It is not always appropriate, of course, for work to be done in teams. But when a team structure is employed, and those teams work effectively, many benefits accrue to the organization and to the team members themselves.

Benefits of Teams

- Increased creativity, problem solving, and innovation.
- Higher-quality decisions.
- Improved processes.
- Global competitiveness.
- Increased quality.
- Improved communication.
- Reduced turnover and absenteeism and increased employee morale.

- *Increased creativity, problem solving, and innovation:* Bringing together a group of individuals who possess a wealth of ideas, perspectives, knowledge, and skills can result in a synergy through which new ideas can be entertained. We each have a unique set of skills. Working with others allows us to combine our skills and talents to create new approaches to solving problems.[9] An example is a team of marketers where each person applies his or her strengths to the issue at hand. One person who is very creative can lead the process of coming up with ideas; another who is detail-oriented can do the initial research; a third person who is skilled in graphic applications can put together a great sales presentation.

- *Higher-quality decisions:* Teamwork enhances the quality of the outcomes. Teamwork involves the collective effort of a group of people who represent diverse backgrounds and experiences. As more ideas are produced and alternatives are considered, the team gets closer to optimal decisions—decisions that are stronger because they have been made with various perspectives and interests in mind.

- *Improved processes:* Teamwork results in a systematic approach to problem solving. Because of the necessary coordination between and transfer of learning among team members, teamwork results in organized approaches to the situation at hand. For example, a team is more likely than an individual to set up project checkpoints and planning systems to enable all team members to contribute to the project as it unfolds. Teamwork also permits distribution of workloads for faster and more efficient handling of large tasks or problems.[10] When members representing different organizations work together to improve a process that cuts across multiple organizational functions, more glitches and interdependencies will be uncovered and addressed than would be by individuals working independently.

■ *Global competitiveness:* Teamwork enables companies to compete globally. Firms in the United States are relying increasingly on diverse teams to compete in the global economy.[11] Diverse teams have skill sets and perspectives that are superior to what a single individual can bring to the table. For example, when Clairol marketed its popular Mist Stick in parts of Germany, it flopped. Had the Clairol marketing team included someone of German origin, they could have informed the group that *mist* was a slang word for "manure." As we continue developing and marketing our products in a global marketplace, combining diverse perspectives is essential.

■ *Increased quality:* Studies show that those large, complex, global companies that have moved to teams show increases in productivity, employee ownership of and accountability for their work, timeliness, efficiency, and customer service.[12] This results in higher-quality standards than are possible when individuals or groups of individuals, who lack a common goal, are doing the work.

■ *Improved communication:* The use of teams in the workplace enhances employee communication. In a traditional, hierarchical organization, communication tends to flow primarily in one direction—downward. In a team-based organization, communication flows laterally, upward, downward, and even outside the organization's boundaries (e.g., customers and suppliers). Teamwork requires collective action that is grounded in words and actions. It's not sufficient for one person to determine how he or she wants to work. Each person must get others on board before proceeding. In effective teams, there is rich sharing of information and ideas that improves communication within the team and between the team and the organization.[13]

■ *Reduced turnover and absenteeism and increased employee morale:* Teamwork results in changes in employee behaviors and attitudes. Teamwork fosters a camaraderie that helps many employees to feel more a part of the organization than when working independently. They feel ownership of the problems on which they work, get immediate feedback from teammates, see the fruits of their labors, and feel they have an impact on their job and the organization. Compared with the alienation employees often experience in traditional firms, employees in team-based organizations are happier, more committed, and more loyal to their organization.

The chart below contains examples of the positive outcomes that resulted when organizations embraced and encouraged team-based work:

Examples of Successes by Self-managed Teams[14]

Organization	Reported Successes
Harley-Davidson	Returned to profitability in six years.
Hallmark	200 percent reduction in design time. Introducing 23,000 new card lines each year.
Liberty Mutual	50 percent reduction in contract process time. Saving of more than $50 million per year.
Johns Hopkins Hospital	Patient volume increased by 21 percent. Turnover reduced, absenteeism reduced by 20 percent.
Monsanto	Quality and productivity improved by 47 percent in 4 years.
Saab and Volvo	4 percent increase in production output. Inventory turnover increased from 9 to 21 times a year.

Potential Limitations of Teams

While this chapter focuses primarily on the effectiveness of teams and work groups and how-tos for being a productive team member, there are some concerns about teams and their ability to make the most effective decisions. Some of these concerns are expressed briefly below.

Limitations of Teams

- **Groupthink. Groupthink**[15]—or individuals agreeing reluctantly with a group's decision—is a potential problem for teams. Groupthink can happen when a decision is made in a hurry, when one or a few members are extremely dominant in a group setting, or when one or more members present believe they haven't had a chance to air their concerns before an action is taken.
- **Social loafing.** By definition a team is a collection of three or more people. Invariably, a team will be composed of members with different work ethics and work styles, and this can result in some individuals doing more work than others.
- *Quality concerns.* Ironically, although there is much evidence that teams produce quality outcomes, the fact is that some individuals have the expert knowledge necessary to be able to make decisions independently without the benefit of a team.
- *Timeliness.* Individuals can make decisions more quickly than teams, especially if gaining buy-in from others is not an essential component of the action under consideration.
- *Diversity.* In general, diversity of background and thought process is a good way to ensure that multiple perspectives will be incorporated into a particular decision. Sometimes, especially when expedience is desired or when management has a clear preference for a particular course of action, a homogenous group can make decisions more quickly and easily than can a more diverse group.

Organizing work into teams is the wave of the future. In fact, many organizations now have "virtual teams," in which much or all of the work is done by group members who may be dispersed geographically and communicate with each other primarily via e-mail and the Internet. But like any new phenomenon, it is important to understand that teams have both upsides and downsides. Teams may not be optimal for every business situation. When you are placed in a team, be aware of the potential problems and develop strategies early on to overcome these challenges.

Types of Teams

In the same way sports teams differ in function, makeup, and ultimate goal or purpose, so do teams in the workplace. The more commonly used team types are described below.

Cross-functional Teams: These include members from various departments or business specialties such as marketing, information systems, communications, public relations, operations, human resources, accounting, finance, planning, research and development, and legal. Cross-functional teams are usually charged with developing new products or investigating and improving a companywide problem such as the need to increase speed and efficiency across departmental lines or the need to adopt a new companywide computer system. Cross-functional teams derive their strength from diversity. By including representatives from all or most of an organization's primary functional areas, the team can diagnose a problem from multiple perspectives simultaneously, ensuring that all relevant points of view are taken into account. This can speed up the problem-solving process and result in an outcome that the various departments affected by the change more readily accept.

Case in point: Prior to producing its LH line of cars, Chrysler followed what most would call a serial design process. Engineering would design a car and throw it over the wall to manufacturing. "We can't build this," manufacturing replied, and sent it back over the wall to engineering. This would continue for months or years until marketing was charged with marketing a car that no one wanted. From product inception to market, this process could take as long as six years or more. By that time, technologies were obsolete and other companies easily stole market share. Realizing this, Chrysler moved to a simultaneous, cross-functional team-based design process. Everyone who had a stake in or was affected by the design of a new product was on a team that hashed it out—together. This included people from marketing, sales, engineering, design, and many others. These meetings had conflict, but the conflict was actually helpful. Chrysler was able to reduce the cycle time from over six years to less than 18 months!

Another example of a cross-functional team is a top management team. In many large organizations, the CEO typically makes strategic decisions in collaboration with the leaders of the major functional areas. Even at this level in the organization, top management recognizes their individual strengths and weaknesses and the value that diverse perspectives can add when making key organizational decisions.

Self-managed Teams: These are "groups of employees who are responsible for a complete, self-contained package of responsibilities that relate either to a final product or an ongoing process."[16] Also known as self-directed, self-maintained, or self-regulating, self-managed teams are typically given a charge by senior management and then are given virtually complete discretion over how, when, and what to do to attain their objective. Self-managed teams are expected to coordinate their work without ongoing direction from a supervisor or manager. Self-managed teams set their own norms, make their own planning schedules, set up ways to keep relevant members and others informed of their progress, determine how the work is going to be accomplished, and are held accountable for their end product or "deliverable." Many of these teams are responsible for hiring, training, and firing team members. The flattening of organizational structures, resulting in less hierarchy and fewer managers, makes self-directed teams a popular concept in business today. Of course, it's not as if management flips a switch and a team becomes self-managing. It's a long process of team building and teamwork combined with sufficiently greater responsibility and accountability gained through the team's demonstrated capabilities and performance.

Task Force: This is an ad hoc, temporary project team assembled to develop a product, service, or system or to solve a specific problem or set of problems. Companies are always faced with the challenge of getting ongoing, day-to-day work done while utilizing available resources to work on various change processes or product innovations. For example, a technology company might designate a group to study the next wave in software development while others are maintaining and servicing existing software programs. Often task force members are individuals who have demonstrated interest or skill in the area being examined by the task force, so the members are enthusiastic about the project and its potential. The task force process is very common in business today. It is lower in cost than hiring an outside consultant or group of contract workers and allows for management to allocate resources at will to various projects as the needs of the company and the interests of its employees change.

Process Improvement Teams: These teams focus on specific methods, operations, or procedures and are assembled with the specific goal of enhancing the particular component being studied. Process improvement teams are typically composed of individuals with expertise and experience in the process being reviewed. They are assigned the tasks of eliminating redundant steps, looking for ways to reduce costs, identifying ways to improve quality, or finding means for providing quicker, better customer service.[17] Process improvement teams are often given training on problem-solving tools and techniques to help them map processes, identify root causes of problems, and prioritize potential solutions.

To analyze a system and make recommendations for changes, process improvement team members diagnose the current state of a process and chart how it occurs step by step. They review customer or internal data and collect data from other sources such as managers, competitors, and others as needed. They identify ways the process can be enhanced, make their recommendations, and sometimes assist the operating units involved in implementing the changes. Process improvement teams are usually temporary and disband once the process being studied has been changed to the satisfaction of management.

Team Developmental Stages

Groups typically pass through a series of stages as they grow and evolve into teams. Theorists postulate that a team goes in and out of at least five stages in its life cycle:[18] forming, storming, norming, performing, adjourning. This process is fluid—teams may revisit a stage, or skip one or more altogether. Each phase has distinguishing characteristics and presents particular challenges to team members and their managers.

Stage One—Forming

In this stage, a team is established to accomplish a particular task. Typically the group members will not know each other, and even if they do, there is a feeling of uncertainty and tentativeness because people haven't had a chance yet to get to know one another and set group objectives.[19] In the **forming** stage, members will engage in behaviors such as defining the initial assignment, discussing how to divvy up the necessary tasks, understanding the broad scope and objectives of the project, and learning about the resources (time, equipment, personnel) available to the team as it works to complete the project. In this stage, there is some testing by members of leadership roles, some discovery of personality similarities and differences, some initial disclosure, and usually relatively little progress on the task.

As a team member or team leader, your role in stage one is to encourage the group to establish its mission and purpose, set up a work schedule, get to know one another, and establish some initial norms for working together.

Stage Two—Storming

In this stage, a group experiences differences over factors such as direction, leadership, work style and approach, and perceptions about the expected quality and state of the end product or deliverable. As is true of any relationship, conflict is inevitable. Many couples feel bad when they experience their first fight, and teams are no exception. When the first conflict among group members emerges, some or all of the members begin to feel less enthusiastic about the group and might even doubt the group can come together and achieve its objective. There may be struggles over leadership ("my way is best"), power ("if you don't agree we'll leave you behind") and roles ("who appointed you chief?"). In the **storming** stage, feelings emerge such as resistance to the task or approach being taken by the group, resentment about differences in workload, anger about roles and responsibilities, and changes in attitude about the group or toward individual group members and concerns. Typically in the storming stage, the group is in conflict and chaos, as the group has not yet established ways to communicate about these differences. During this stage, few if any processes and procedures are in place, as the need for them wasn't anticipated due to the lack of prior conflict. All of this can result in arguing among members, emergence of subgroups, and disunity. If and when a group in which you are working enters this stage, what can you do?

In the storming stage, your role as a group member or leader is to refrain from taking sides. Encourage the group to develop communication channels. Help your group members focus on the task and not on personal differences. Promote an environment of open communication to ensure that the inevitable conflict is healthy and results in improved communication and commitment to the group's task. Remember that an appropriate level of tension motivates a team, but too much or too little can affect productivity.[20] If your group cannot resolve or work effectively with conflict, request the assistance of a trained process consultant or facilitator. A group that can't learn how to handle conflict may never achieve its deliverable.

Stage Three—Norming

In this stage, the group faces its issues, conflicts, and power and leadership struggles openly and directly. The members establish and adhere to patterns of acceptable behavior and learn to incorporate new methods and procedures into their working together. In the **norming** stage, members feel a new ability to express constructive criticism; they feel part of a working team and a sense of relief that everything will work out.[21] In this stage, members attempt to achieve harmony by avoiding unnecessary conflict, acting more friendly toward and trusting of each other, and developing a sense of team unity ("together, we can solve this"). Norms don't have to be established about every single decision or policy, only those that are particularly significant to team members.[22]

As a team member or leader, your role is to encourage team members to take on more responsibility, work together to create means acceptable for solving problems, set challenging goals, and take personal responsibility for team success. As a leader, you set the tone. Don't expect others to "do as you say, but not as you do." If you are seen bickering with colleagues and secretly plotting political moves, team members are less likely to emulate the helpful norming behaviors and may regress to the storming stage.

Stage Four—Performing

In the **performing** stage, teams have worked through their differences. Their membership is stable, the task is clear, and eyes are on the prize. Team members are highly motivated to accomplish their task and focused on team objectives rather than individual interests. Through working closely together, team members have developed insights into each other's strengths and weaknesses (many even finish each other's sentences), feel satisfied with the team's progress, and believe the team will successfully reach or even exceed its goals. In this stage, members engage in constructive self-change for the good of the group; experience greatly enhanced ability to communicate with and give feedback to each other; are able to anticipate, prevent, or work through group problems; and, as a result, develop a close attachment to the team.[23]

As a team member or leader, your role at this stage is to encourage members to provide support to and serve as resources for each other. Make sure the team continues with its progress and maintains its cohesion and morale, and guide it toward success. Do remain vigilant, however. It's easy to kick back and relax, believing that once a team gets to this phase of development, it stays there. That may or may not be true. Changes in membership, scope of the task, or broader organizational changes can cause a team to regress developmentally. In addition, the close attachments members have to a team could possibly blind them to other developing problems.

Stage Five—Adjourning

After successfully completing the task or objective, teams may disband permanently or take a temporary break. Some may get new members or receive a new objective. This stage is usually brought on by an imminent deadline. At the **adjourning** stage, members are likely to feel disappointment—if the experience was positive—or gratitude—if the experience was negative. The task at this stage is to tie up loose ends and complete final follow-up on projects.

As a team member or leader, your role at this end stage is to encourage the team members to debrief the project, discussing the lessons learned that members can take with them to new projects and convey to new teams tackling similar issues. It is also helpful at this stage to recognize the team for its efforts. This could take the form of public recognition (a blurb on the team's accomplishments in the monthly newsletter), a reward (some organizations reward teams with a percentage of the savings or revenues realized as a result of the team's work), or other benefit (use company funds to take the team out for lunch). By providing encouragement and recognizing accomplishments, hard work, and efforts, you help to continue momentum and build motivation.[24] Of course, ongoing work project teams may not physically adjourn. They may remain intact, continuing with a new set of objectives once a particular project is complete. In this case, rather than adjourning, the team members may choose to debrief at certain checkpoints along the way, evaluating their processes and communication efforts to ensure they're keeping current and are as productive as they can be.

It is healthy for groups to move through some or all of these stages as they evolve into a team. Not all groups go through all the stages, and some go through them at different paces. For example, if a group's members knew each other previously and had similar values and goals—as well as a tight deadline—they might be able to move almost immediately to the norming stage. In another case, where the group members don't know each other well and they have some time before the deliverable is due, they might take longer to reach the norming phase and coalesce as a real team just before the deliverable is due. Some may get stuck in one of the stages and disband before progressing to the next stage or perform at a lower level than what might have been possible. A group stuck in the storming stage but facing an imminent deadline has to continue performing. In this case, it is likely that its performance will suffer due to the inability to function cohesively. In some extreme cases, a group will be dysfunctional and will require outside intervention in order to complete its task. As is true with relationships, teams have developmental cycles. Understanding this ahead of time can help you develop strategies for helping your group evolve into a team and to increase its effectiveness every step of the way.

Characteristics of High-Performance Teams

As former Notre Dame coach Lou Holtz said, "Winning is never accidental. To win consistently you must have a clear plan and intense motivation." As we have said, not all teams are alike. As a team member or leader, your primary goal is to encourage your group to evolve into a motivated, goal-oriented, successful team; we refer to these types of teams as high-performance teams. In **high-performance teams,** there is a commitment to quality and a dedication to producing the best outcome possible. Research shows that most high-performance work teams possess the following characteristics:[25]

- *Common purpose and goals:* High-performing teams have a clearly defined mission, purpose, and goals. Individual team members understand why the team has been formed and what is expected from the team.[26]
- *Intention:* According to researcher Barry Ekman, the best teams are not ad-hoc or unstructured. Instead, they are planned or structured to achieve a specific goal or address a specific challenge. In structured team building, the importance is on intentionally striving to achieve sustainable outcomes by matching team psychology with change and technology.[27]
- *Clear roles:* High-performing teams have clarity about roles and responsibilities. Team members understand their roles and assignments and how they impact the group, have clear and stable boundaries, are aware of how their work affects other members, and know the direction that is needed to get there.[28]
- *Communication processes:* High-performing teams have extensive communication mechanisms. They communicate regularly with each other either in person, via telephone, or through e-mail and keep those unable to attend meetings informed of the group's progress. They constantly update their planning calendar and communicate about adjustments, as they are needed.[29]
- *Accepting and supportive leadership:* Studies have found that team leaders who function more as coaches than managers facilitate the development of participative, motivated teams.[30] These leaders were proactive and committed to the team, and they provided encouraging, positive influence over the team and its members. A manager pulls a group along; a coach gently pushes it from behind. A manager works to maintain control; a coach works to give up control.[31]
- *Small size:* The size of the team can be essential to a team's success. The optimal size is between 6 and 10. This is large enough to accomplish the work and provide enough human resources and ideas, and small enough for a team to coalesce and reach consensus on major issues.[32]
- *High levels of technical and interpersonal skills:* High-performing teams are composed of members who have a breadth of both specialty and people skills. Understanding how to work with and through others, problem solving, managing project work flow, giving and receiving feedback, goal setting, time management, and conflict management are some of the most valuable skills in team settings.[33]
- *Open relationships and trust:* In high-performing teams, the members develop cooperative behaviors including understanding what is needed from one another; defining the interrelated activities necessary to complete the project; volunteering to assist each other in doing what's needed; and completing assigned tasks competently, on time, accurately, and with quality. Trust is built through behaviors such as being dependable, doing what is agreed upon, being kept informed and informing others of necessary facts and information, keeping confidential information private, and allowing others to use their specialized knowledge and abilities.[34]

■ *Accountability:* High-performance team members understand for what (and to what degree) they and others are held accountable. The team receives the message from the organization that performance matters—that it makes a difference whether goals are achieved or not. Expectations are clarified, and members are held responsible as individuals as well as members of the team.[35]

■ *Reward structures:* High-performing teams are rewarded for team accomplishments in addition to individual recognition. Organizations that support the team concept organize their recruiting, training, development, sales, business development, strategic planning, compensation, performance appraisal, and promotion strategies to support and reward teamwork.[36] When these strategies don't match with or undermine team processes or philosophies, the organization sends a mixed message and members find ways to "game" the system—often at the expense of their team. If an individual team member who "saves the day" for the department is rewarded for individual behavior, it sends the message that collaboration is not as valued as individual contributions or heroics, even if management's rhetoric suggests teams are truly valued.

Tips for Effective Teams

As a member of a team, it is important to be self-directed and work for the betterment of your team. You and your team members will be working with minimal supervision, and it is everyone's responsibility to make the team work. As athletes have learned, if one team member doesn't come through, the quality and performance of the entire team is affected. Teamwork requires full dedication and participation by all members of the team.

The following tips can help make your next team experience more positive and successful.

■ *Be focused.* Cooperate with your team members in concentrating on the current issues they face. Cooperation builds trust and mutual respect. Be willing and dedicated to working toward the common purpose.

■ *Handle conflict directly* and be willing to compromise. Be willing to explore conflict in a constructive, win–win fashion. Stand up for things that are important to you, but don't insist on getting your way in every discussion. When working together, put personalities aside and confront issues that arise. Resolve conflicts and walk away from sessions with regard, respect, and esteem for yourself and your team members.[37]

■ *Focus on both process and content.* Pay attention to the *process* of becoming and working together as a team as well as the *result* or end goal expected from the team. Teamwork is more than producing a deliverable. It also entails the approach or process used when people are working together.[38] The ends don't necessarily justify the means if team members despise and lack respect for team members because of the way decisions and outcomes were rammed through when teams fail to use a consensus approach. At team meetings, review both the processes being used as well as the status of the project.

■ *Actively participate,* and encourage others to do the same. At the beginning of a project, talk about roles and responsibilities. Also talk frankly about team members' schedules and their availability to participate fully in the project. Set up checkpoints to ensure that all are contributing equally.

■ *Keep sensitive issues private.* At the beginning of a project, discuss the importance of confidentiality. All teams engage in discussions that could be hurtful if made public. Have a pact that private information and views shared will be just that—not relayed to others outside the group. "What's said in the room, stays in the room."

■ *Communicate openly and positively.* In order to have full team participation, and for the team to learn and develop, it is essential that team members do not embarrass, reject, mock, or punish someone for speaking up and sharing ideas and perceptions. Foster a climate of psychological safety in order to motivate members to participate, admit errors, and share ideas and beliefs openly and comfortably.[39]

■ *Take time to establish operating guidelines* and clarify expectations. Make sure everyone is present for initial discussions of roles, responsibilities, and operating guidelines. For these guidelines to work, it is best that everyone participate in establishing and agreeing to uphold them. Put them in writing and have everyone sign them.

■ *Monitor what's going on with the team.* Watch for reactions, nonverbal cues, level of participation (or lack thereof), and general changes in the group's dynamics. Develop observational skills to help the team reach its full potential. A side benefit of doing this is that you increase your own interpersonal skills as you try to set a tone that is conducive to all members enjoying and participating in the team experience.[40]

■ *Practice giving (and receiving) effective feedback.* Express support and acceptance by praising and seeking other members' ideas and conclusions. If you disagree with others' viewpoints, criticize ideas but not the people. Be specific about the ideas that concern you and accept others' concerns about your ideas.

■ *Work with underperformers* to keep them in the flow of the project and prevent them from becoming excluded from the group.[41] If slackers are an issue in your team, talk with them immediately, preferably one on one. Find out if there is a personal problem preventing the member from being more engaged. Offer to be supportive but don't carry the workload. Give that team member specific, manageable tasks and hold him or her accountable. If the underperformance continues, talk with your manager or instructor. The person may need to be removed from the group or reassigned to a different team.

■ *Energize the team* when motivation is low by suggesting new ideas, through humor or use of enthusiasm. Encourage a time-out, if one is needed, or suggest a work or coffee break.

■ *Be reliable and conscientious.* Respect other members by honoring deadlines, commitments, and project milestones.[42] If you are having difficulty making a deadline, don't wait until the last minute—discuss the problem immediately with a team member or with the team. There might be a different way of approaching it. It's easier for a team to be flexible when there is adequate time to review the situation and come up with a different plan.

■ *When needed, give direction to the team's work* by stating and restating the purpose of assignments, setting or calling attention to time limits, and offering procedures on how to complete the assignment most effectively.

■ *Be supportive of your team members.* Always ask how you can help. It's a great way to remind everyone you're a team with collective objectives, not a group of individual contributors competing against each other.

Why Teams Fail

A note of caution: for teams and teamwork to succeed, there must be ample time in which to complete an assignment. Also needed are adequate resources to achieve the stated objectives and full management support of the team's effort. While the concept of teamwork is prevalent in both work and nonwork settings, not all situations warrant or are conducive to teams. Teams may be faced with tight deadlines; merging of processes and responsibilities; technological challenges; mismatched skills and abilities; unresolvable personality clashes, styles, and behaviors; limited work or teaming experience; or power struggles. In these situations, or in cases where there is no interdependence or need for collaboration, teamwork is going to be difficult if not impossible. These issues should be addressed early so that modifications can be made if necessary.

For example, if a team lacks the proper skill sets, additional members or training sessions can be added. If a power struggle is unfolding, a facilitator can be appointed. Inexperienced team members can be assigned informal mentors or coaches. Sometimes, if it's in the best interests of an organization, a team can be disbanded altogether. Perhaps the mission wasn't clearly defined at the outset of a project and the team members find they are unable to devote the time necessary to do the job. Or perhaps management requested individuals to work on a team project but made no allowances for mandatory day-to-day tasks. In situations such as these, it's appropriate for the team to be reconfigured (or disbanded) so that the original objective can be attained through either a different team or a different approach. Oftentimes, teams ignore early problems—perhaps believing such problems can be overcome—and become dysfunctional.[43] Intervening early, in a proactive way, can turn a team around or cause the organization to consider other, non-team-based approaches to solving a problem.

How can you deal with team members who aren't performing? Following are some tips.

Dealing with Problem Team Members

■ **Absentee member:** A member can become distracted by a work or personal problem that prevents him or her from following through on commitments made to the team. In this case, the best strategy is to be direct immediately. Discuss the situation with the team member in a way in which the person does not feel he or she is being put on the defensive. Explain the problem and find out the team member's perception of the situation. Ask specifically if the team member still has the time necessary for the team. If not, part ways if possible. If this is not possible, determine a way for the team member to make contributions outside of the normal meeting times and make the person accountable for a specific segment of the work that limits reliance on the team.

■ **Social loafer:** As mentioned earlier, it is not uncommon for one or more persons on a team to be able to "hide" the fact they're not contributing. This typically happens when the team members' work ethics differ and one or more team members "step up to the plate" and take on additional responsibility to ensure the work gets done, effectively covering for the less productive team members. Work standards will always vary from person to person. A strategy for dealing with this is to raise the issue at the onset of the project. Divide the responsibilities and set up checkpoints to ensure each member is contributing roughly equally. If a discrepancy appears, try to quantify it and re-allocate the workload so all members are contributing roughly equally.

■ **Procrastinator:** We're all human, and a seemingly human tendency is to "put off until tomorrow what we should be working on today." This is particularly problematic for work teams. Teams are composed of individuals with different work schedules and work styles. Some people thrive on the pressure of imminent deadlines while others find waiting until the last minute to be overly stressful. In this situation it is best to do two things: (a) set up interim checkpoints, or minideadlines, to ensure the work progresses at a reasonable pace, and (b) be realistic when work schedules are drawn up and deadlines determined. Prior to establishing deadlines, ask all team members to check personal and work calendars to catch any problems before they occur. At each meeting reclarify the commitments that might affect a person's inability to adhere to a deadline set earlier. And build in some slack: set the final deadline for a few days before the *actual* deadline—just in case!

Teams may not be a cure for all that ails an organization. But, teams can be very effective if the team structure makes sense and members practice the suggestions outlined in the chapter. Other steps team members and their managers can take to improve the likelihood of team success are summarized in the chart below:

Tips for Managing for Outstanding Results

■ Care about the people you work with—understand them, know what's important to them, and be able to motivate them.

■ Don't worry about who gets the credit—emphasize team effort and rewards; use the "whatever is best for the team" approach.

■ Respect individual differences—accept individuals and work to emphasize strengths and minimize weaknesses.

■ Subordinate yourself to a higher purpose—keep the common goal in the forefront.

■ Know yourself—be aware of your strengths and admit your weaknesses; surround yourself with people who can compensate for your weaknesses.

■ Don't be afraid to follow—some of the best teams are those where the leader doesn't call all the shots.

Source: Stephen Covey, "Team Up for a Superstar Office," *USA Weekend*, Sept. 4–6, 1998, p. 10.

Summary

Workplaces in the United States and abroad have embraced teaming. This is no accident. Organizations that implemented work teams as a way to improve products, services, and processes have witnessed tremendous measurable benefits. Some of these benefits accrue because of synergies—the notion that teams produce more and better solutions than individuals—gained from combining various skill sets, perspectives, abilities, and work styles on a single team. Not all teams produce phenomenal outcomes. By understanding the normal phases of group development and ways to gain and maintain group productivity and motivation, you can help your teams reach their full potential.

Key Terms and Concepts

Absentee member	Performing
Adjourning	Process improvement team
Cross-functional teams	Procrastinator
Forming	Self-managed team
Group	Social loafing/loafer
Groupthink	Storming
High-performance team	Task force
Norming	Team

Endnotes

1. Quote by Tracey Edwards in "Teaming with Talent," by Jim White, *Management Today,* Sept. 1999, p. 56.

2. Lillian Chaney and Julie Lyden, "Making U.S. Teams Work," *Supervision,* Jan. 2000, p. 6.

3. Karl L. Smart and Carol Barnum, "Communication in Cross-Functional Teams: An Introduction to This Special Issue," *Technical Communication,* Feb. 2000, p. 19.

4. Kevin McManus, "Do You Have Teams?" *IIE Solutions,* April 2000, p. 21.

5. Jim White, "Teaming with Talent," *Management Today,* Sept. 1999, p. 56.

6. Harvey Mackay, "Get on the Team and Be a Winner," *Providence Business News,* August 16, 1999, p. 38.

7. Chaney and Lyden, "Making U.S. Teams Work."

8. McManus, "Do You Have Teams?"

9. Ibid.

10. Smart and Barnum, "Communication in Cross-Functional Teams."

11. Chaney and Lyden, "Making U.S. Teams Work."

12. Mohsen Attaran and Tai T. Nguyen, "Succeeding with Self-managed Work Teams," *Industrial Management,* July–August 1999, p. 24.

13. Larry Cole and Michael Scott Cole, "Teamwork is Spelled Incorrectly: Teamwork = Communication," *Communication World,* April 2000, p. 56.

14. Attaran and Nguyen, "Succeeding with Self-managed Work Teams." Reprinted by permission of the Institute of Industrial Engineers, 25 Technology Park, Norcross, GA 30092, 770–449–0461. Copyright © 1999.

15. Irving I. Janis, *Groupthink,* 2nd ed. (Boston, MA: Houghton-Mifflin, 1982).

16. Attaran and Nguyen, "Succeeding with Self-managed Work Teams."

17. David Rohlander, "Building High-Performance Teams," *Credit Union Executive,* March 2000, p. 36.

18. Bruce W. Tuckman, "Developmental Sequences in Small Groups," *Psychological Bulletin* 63 (1965), pp. 384–99. The stage theory of team development was first identified by Tuckerman. Subsequent research has found the stages occur in a slightly different order. While the original model is reflected in this chapter, some researchers have found that teams more likely progress through conforming before entering the storming stage. See R. E. Quinn and K. S. Cameron, "Organizational Life Cycles and Shifting Criteria of Effectiveness," *Management Science* 29 (1983), pp. 37–61. Also see K. S. Cameron and D. A. Whetten, "Perceptions of Organizational Effectiveness in Organizational Life Cycles," *Administrative Science Quarterly* 27 (1981), pp. 525–44.

19. Peter R. Scholtes, *The Team Handbook* (Madison, WI: Joiner and Associates, 1988).

20. John R. Myers, "What It Takes to Make a Team," *Purchasing,* Sept. 2, 1999, p. 91.

21. Scholtes, *The Team Handbook.*

22. Daniel C. Feldman, "The Development and Enforcement of Group Norms," *Academy of Management Review* 9, no.1 (1984), pp. 47–53.

23. Scholtes, *The Team Handbook.*

24. Rona Leach, "Supervision: From Me to We," *Supervision,* Feb. 2000, p. 8.

25. Ruth Wageman, "Critical Success Factors for Creating Superb Self-Managing Teams," *Organizational Dynamics,* Summer 1997, p. 49.

26. Rohlander, "Building High-Performance Teams."

27. Barry Ekman and Emmanuela Ginngregorio, "Establishing Truly Peak Performance Teams—Beyond Metaphoric Challenges," *Human Resource Management International Digest,* 11, no. 3 (2003), p. 2.

28. American Management Association, "HR Update: Creating Real Teamwork at the Top," *HR Focus,* Jan. 2000, p. 2.

29. Smart and Barnum, "Communication in Cross-Functional Teams."

30. Paulo Vieira Cunha and Maria Joao Louro, "Building Teams That Learn," *The Academy of Management Executive,* Feb. 2000, p. 152.

31. Renee Evenson, "Team Effort: Beyond Employees to Team, beyond Manager to Coach," *Supervision,* Feb. 2000, p. 11.

32. Chaney and Lyden, "Making U.S. Teams Work."

33. Avan R. Jassawalla and Hemant C. Sashittal, "Building Collaborative Cross-Functional New Product Teams," *The Academy of Management Executive,* August 1999, p. 50.

34. Cole and Cole, "Teamwork Is Spelled Incorrectly."

35. Russ Forrester and Allan B. Drexler, "A Model for Team-Based Organizational Performance," *The Academy of Management Executive,* August 1999, p. 36.

36. Becky L. Nichol, "Top Ten Reasons Teams Become Dysfunctional," *National Public Accountant,* Feb. 2000, p. 12.

37. Jassawalla and Sashittal, "Building Collaborative Cross-Functional New Product Teams."

38. Cole and Cole, "Teamwork Is Spelled Incorrectly."

39. Cunha and Louro, "Building Teams."

40. Myers, "What It Takes to Make a Team."

41. Ted Gautschi, "Strengthen Your Team," *Design News,* Oct. 18, 1999, p. 158.

42. Myers, "What It Takes to Make a Team."

43. Smart and Barnum, "Communication in Cross-Functional Teams."

Exercise 10–A **Bridge Building**	Groups of four to six are tasked with creating a bridge out of the materials provided. You have 30 minutes in which to complete this task. When the project is complete or time is called—whichever comes first—your instructor will roll a ball across your bridge to ensure it meets the project specifications. Following this activity, discuss these questions in your group.

Questions

1. How did your group decide how to build the bridge? Did it make a plan or did it just start building?
2. Did anyone play a leadership role in the task? Explain.
3. What made building the bridge as a group, rather than as an individual, more difficult?
4. In what ways did the group make the project easier? Explain.
5. Was your group a group or team? Explain.

Exercise 10–B **The Story: A Team** **Exercise**	Read the instructions and story below and answer the corresponding questions. Next, complete the same task in your assigned group.

What Does the Story Tell?

Instructions

Read the following story and take for granted that everything it says is true. Read carefully because, in spots, the story is deliberately vague. Don't try to memorize it since you can look back at it at any time.

Then read the numbered statements about the story and decide whether you consider each one true, false, or questionable. Circling the "T" means you feel sure the statement is definitely true. Circling the "F" means you feel sure the statement is definitely false. Circling the "?" means you cannot tell whether it is true or false. If you feel doubtful about any part of a statement, circle the question mark.

Take the statements in turn and do not go back later to change any of your answers. Do not reread any of the statements after you have answered them.

Story

The owner of the Adams Manufacturing Company entered the office of one of his foremen where he found three employees playing cards. One of them was Carl Young, brother-in-law of foreman Henry Dilson. Dilson, incidentally, often worked late. Company rules did not specifically forbid gambling on the premises, but the president had expressed himself forcibly on the subject.

Statements about the Story

1.	In brief, the story is about a company owner who found three men playing cards.	T	F	?
2.	The president walked into the office of one of his foremen.	T	F	?
3.	Company rules forbade playing cards on the premises after hours.	T	F	?
4.	While the card playing took place in Henry Dilson's office, the story does not state whether Dilson was present.	T	F	?
5.	Dilson never worked late.	T	F	?
6.	Gambling on the premises of the Adams Manufacturing Company was not punished.	T	F	?
7.	Carl Young was not playing cards when the president walked in.	T	F	?
8.	Three employees were gambling in a foreman's office.	T	F	?
9.	While the card players were surprised when the owner walked in, it is not clear whether they will be punished.	T	F	?
10.	Henry Dilson is Carl Young's brother-in-law.	T	F	?

11. The president is opposed to gambling on company premises.   T   F   ?

12. Carl Young did not take part in the card game in   T   F   ?
Henry Dilson's office.

Questions

1. What process did you use to come up with the group answers?

2. Did anyone act as a leader or facilitator in the exercise? Explain.

3. In what ways was it difficult to achieve a group decision?

4. Which behaviors blocked the group's process? Which ones helped?

5. What are the advantages or disadvantages of working in a group compared to working as an individual?

Exercise 10–C
Case Study on Gaining Appropriate Membership on Teams

This is the team's third meeting. The team's task, deliverables, and membership have been dictated by a steering committee that oversees the division's teaming efforts. Members represent different areas and management levels within the division. A new team member who missed the first two meetings enters the room. Let's eavesdrop:

SCRIBE: "Okay. Here's our agenda. Does this sound ok to everyone?"

NEW TEAM MEMBER: "Well, not exactly. I have a question regarding the team's task. I know I missed the first two meetings, but I'm unclear about our purpose. I mean, without a well-understood purpose, are we ready to talk about membership? I'm not even sure if I should be here!"

SCRIBE: "Well, I suppose we can add "team purpose" to the agenda. How much time should we allot?"

TEAM LEADER: (Feeling strained by all the necessary structure.) "Could we hold off with the agenda for a few minutes . . . I know we need the agenda, but I think we should talk about purpose for a few minutes at least; then we can get back to the regular agenda. She (the new team member) brings up a good point."

Some discussion ensues. It becomes clear that the team's purpose *is* unclear. Other additional information is revealed, such as the fact that there had been three other team members who, shortly after being appointed by the steering committee, decided to excuse themselves from the team. Also, the team leader brought a new person in (call her Possible New Member), who is not really a full-fledged member until the steering committee approves it.

SCRIBE: "Back to the agenda. Were there any corrections to the minutes? (No response.) Okay, now for today's meeting roles . . . oh, our timekeeper isn't here today."

NEW TEAM MEMBER: (Looking at Possible New Member) "Would you like to keep time?"

TEAM LEADER: "Well, we're not sure if she is an official team member yet. Remember, the steering committee hasn't okayed her yet. Should she keep time if she's not?"

NEW TEAM MEMBER: "What's the difference? And why do we need the steering committee's blessing? Let's just do it."

TEAM LEADER: "Actually, there are some other names, in addition to Possible Team Member, that we've submitted to the steering committee. After all, we've lost three people since the team began."

NEW TEAM MEMBER: "Do we need additional people? Why? Again, doesn't it depend on what we're trying to accomplish?"

Questions

1. Why is it important to clarify a team's purpose? Once the task is given, why is clarification necessary?

2. What role does this purpose play in defining team membership? Why do you suppose others have "excused themselves" from the team?

3. How effective is the team leader? Explain.

4. Meeting management techniques—using agendas, having a scribe and timekeeper—are intended to make meetings more effective. In what ways could these techniques have the opposite effect?

5. If you were asked to participate in this meeting, what would you do to get the process back on track? Explain.

**Exercise 10–D
The Case of the Take-Charge Team Leader**

You are a member of a team that is meeting for the third time. Your goal is to reduce the number and dollar amount of workers' compensation claims. The team consists of members from safety, human resources, legal, and medical (e.g., staff nurses and doctors) departments. The team leader—a senior level manager—demonstrates a "take-charge" approach in that he or she believes he or she knows more about the task and assignment than anyone on the team. Early in the team's existence, the leader shared a project milestone chart that the team accepted. While the group has kept up with its assignments and is working rather effectively, the team leader seems impatient with the team's progress. In fact, the leader would like to exert greater control over the team's activities because he or she already has supporting data from outside groups and departments about the task and wants to complete the project in record time. However, you and other team members are concerned that (1) there may be other issues that have not yet surfaced, and (2) if his or her ideas are accepted, one of the team members may lose his or her position in the firm.

Questions

1. What issues are at play? How would you feel in this situation?

2. If the leader is so capable, why do you suppose management created a team to address this particular (and highly visible) problem?

3. At this point, what would you do and why?

4. If no changes were made, what do you think the final outcome would be?

**Exercise 10–E
Reflection/Action Plan**

This chapter focused on teams in the workplace—what they are, why they are important, and how to improve your skill in this area. Complete the worksheet below upon completing all the reading and experiential activities for this chapter.

1. The one or two areas in which I am most strong are:

2. The one or two areas in which I need more improvement are:

3. If I did only one thing to improve in this area, it would be to:

A Guide to
Case Analysis

I keep six honest serving men
(They taught me all I knew);
Their names are What and Why and When;
And How and Where and Who.
— *Rudyard Kipling*

In most courses in strategic management, students use cases about actual companies to practice strategic analysis and to gain some experience in the tasks of crafting and implementing strategy. A case sets forth, in a factual manner, the events and organizational circumstances surrounding a particular managerial situation. It puts readers at the scene of the action and familiarizes them with all the relevant circumstances. A case on strategic management can concern a whole industry, a single organization, or some part of an organization; the organization involved can be either profit seeking or not-for-profit. The essence of the student's role in case analysis is to *diagnose* and *size up* the situation described in the case and then to *recommend* appropriate action steps.

Why Use Cases to Practice Strategic Management?

A student of business with tact
Absorbed many answers he lacked.
But acquiring a job,
He said with a sob,
"How does one fit answer to fact?"

The foregoing limerick was used some years ago by Professor Charles Gragg to characterize the plight of business students who had no exposure to cases.[1] The facts are that the mere act of listening to lectures and sound advice about managing does little for anyone's management skills and that the accumulated managerial wisdom cannot effectively be passed on by lectures and assigned readings alone. If anything had been learned about the practice of management, it is that a storehouse of ready-made textbook answers does not exist. Each managerial situation has unique aspects, requiring its own diagnosis, judgment, and tailor-made actions. Cases provide would-be managers with a valuable way to practice wrestling with the actual problems of actual managers in actual companies.

The case approach to strategic analysis is, first and foremost, an exercise in learning by doing. Because cases provide you with detailed information about conditions and problems of different industries and companies, your task of analyzing company after company and situation after situation has the twin benefit of boosting your analytical skills and exposing you to the ways companies and managers actually do things. Most college students have limited managerial backgrounds and only fragmented knowledge about companies and real-life strategic situations. Cases help substitute for on-the-job experience by (1) giving you broader exposure to a variety of industries, organizations, and strategic problems; (2) forcing you to assume a managerial role (as opposed to that of just an onlooker); (3) providing a test of how to apply the tools and techniques of strategic management; and (4) asking you to come up with pragmatic managerial action plans to deal with the issues at hand.

Objectives of Case Analysis

Using cases to learn about the practice of strategic management is a powerful way for you to accomplish five things:[2]

1. *Increase your understanding of what managers should and should not do in guiding a business to success.*

2. *Build your skills in sizing up company resource strengths and weaknesses and in conducting strategic analysis in a variety of industries and competitive situations.*

3. *Get valuable practice in identifying strategic issues that need to be addressed, evaluating strategic alternatives, and formulating workable plans of action.*

4. *Enhance your sense of business judgment, as opposed to uncritically accepting the authoritative crutch of the professor or "back-of-the-book" answers.*

5. *Gaining in-depth exposure to different industries and companies, thereby acquiring something close to actual business experience.*

If you understand that these are the objectives of case analysis, you are less likely to be consumed with curiosity about "the answer to the case." Students who have grown comfortable with and accustomed to textbook statements of fact and definitive lecture notes are often frustrated when discussions about a case do not produce concrete answers. Usually, case discussions produce good arguments for more than one course of action. Differences of opinion nearly always exist. Thus, should a class discussion conclude without a strong, unambiguous consensus on what do to, don't grumble too much when you are *not* told what the answer is or what the company actually did. Just remember that in the business world answers don't come in conclusive black-and-white terms. There are nearly always several feasible courses of action and approaches, each of which may work out satisfactorily. Moreover, in the business world, when one elects a particular course of action, there is no peeking at the back of a book to see if you have chosen the best thing to do and no one to turn to for a provably correct answer. The best test of whether management action is "right" or "wrong" is *results*. If the results of an action turn out to be "good," the decision to take it may be presumed "right." If not, then the action chosen was "wrong" in the sense that it didn't work out.

Hence, the important thing for you to understand about analyzing cases is that the managerial exercise of identifying, diagnosing, and recommending is aimed at building your skills of business judgment. Discovering what the company actually did is no more than frosting on the cake—the actions that company managers actually took may or may not be "right" or best (unless there is accompanying evidence that the results of their actions were highly positive.

The point is this: *The purpose of giving you a case assignment is not to cause you to run to the library or surf the Internet to discover what the company actually did but, rather, to enhance your skills in sizing up situations and developing your managerial judgment about what needs to be done and how to do it.* The aim of case analysis is for *you* to become actively engaged in diagnosing the business issues and managerial problems posed in the case, to propose workable solutions, and to explain and defend your assessments— this is how cases provide you with meaningful practice at being a manager.

Preparing a Case for Class Discussion

If this is your first experience with the case method, you may have to reorient your study habits. Unlike lecture courses where you can get by without preparing intensively for each class and where you have latitude to work assigned readings and reviews of lecture notes into your schedule, a case assignment requires conscientious preparation before class. You will not get much out of hearing the class discuss a case you haven't read, and you certainly won't be able to contribute anything yourself to the discussion. What you have got to do to get ready for class discussion of a case is to study the case, reflect carefully on the situation presented, and develop some reasoned thoughts. Your goal in preparing the case should be to end up with what you think is a sound, well-supported analysis of the situation and a sound, defensible set of recommendations about which managerial actions need to be taken. The Case-TUTOR software downloads that accompany the text and that are available on this same Web site will assist you in preparing the cases— the Case-TUTOR files contain a set of study questions for each case and step-by-step tutorials to walk you through the process of analyzing and developing reasonable recommendations.

To prepare a case for class discussion, we suggest the following approach:

1. ***Skim the case rather quickly to get an overview of the situation it presents.*** This quick overview should give you the general flavor of the situation and indicate the kinds of issues and problems that you will need to wrestle with. If your instructor has provided you with study questions for the case, now is the time to read them carefully.

2. ***Read the case thoroughly to digest the facts and circumstances.*** On this reading, try to gain full command of the situation presented in the case. Begin to develop some tentative answers to the study questions your instructor has provided or that are provided in the Case-TUTOR software package which you can download at the Web site for the text. If your instructor has elected not to give you assignment questions or has elected not to use Case-TUTOR, then start forming your own picture of the overall situation being described.

3. ***Carefully review all the information presented in the exhibits.*** Often, there is an important story in the numbers contained in the exhibits. Expect the information in the case exhibits to be crucial enough to materially affect your diagnosis of the situation.

4. ***Decide what the strategic issues are.*** Until you have identified the strategic issues and problems in the case, you don't know what to analyze, which tools and analytical techniques are called for, or otherwise how to proceed. At times the strategic issues are clear—either being stated in the case or else obvious from reading the case. At other times you will have to dig them out from all the information given; if so, the study questions and the case preparation exercises provided in the Case-TUTOR software will guide you.

5. ***Start your analysis of the issues with some number crunching.*** A big majority of strategy cases call for some kind of number crunching—calculating assorted financial ratios to check out the company's financial condition and recent performance, calculating growth rates of sales or profits or unit volume, checking out profit margins and the makeup of the cost structure, and understanding whatever revenue-cost-profit relationships are present. See Table 1 for a summary of key financial ratios, how they are calculated, and what they show.

6. ***Apply the concepts and techniques of strategic analysis you have been studying.*** Strategic analysis is not just a collection of opinions; rather, it entails applying the concepts and analytical tools described in Chapters 1 through 13 to cut beneath the surface and produce sharp insight and understanding. Every case assigned is strategy related and presents you with an opportunity to usefully apply what you have learned. Your instructor is looking for you to demonstrate that you know *how* and *when* to use the material presented in the text chapters. The case preparation guides on Case-TUTOR will point you toward the proper analytical tools needed to analyze the case situation.

7. ***Check out conflicting opinions and make some judgments about the validity of all the data and information provided.*** Many times cases report views and contradictory opinions (after all, people don't always agree on things, and different people see the same things in different ways). Forcing you to evaluate the data and information presented in the case helps you develop your powers of inference and judgment. Asking you to resolve conflicting information "comes with the territory" because a great many managerial situations entail opposing points of view, conflicting trends, and sketchy information.

8. ***Support your diagnosis and opinions with reasons and evidence.*** The most important things to prepare for are your answers to the question "Why?" For instance, if after studying the case you are of the opinion that the company's managers are doing a poor job, then it is your answer to "Why?" that establishes just how good your analysis of the situation is. If your instructor has provided you with specific study questions for the case or if you are attempting to complete any one of the case preparation exercises on Case-TUTOR, by all means prepare answers that include all the reasons and number-crunching evidence you can muster

to support your diagnosis. Work through the case preparation exercises on Case-TUTOR *conscientiously* or, if you are using study questions provided by the instructor, *generate at least two pages of notes!*

9. ***Develop an appropriate action plan and set of recommendations.*** Diagnosis divorced from corrective action is sterile. The test of a manager is always to convert sound analysis into sound actions—actions that will produce the desired results. Hence, the final and most telling step in preparing a case is to develop an action agenda for management that lays out a set of specific recommendations on what to do. Bear in mind that proposing realistic, workable solutions is far preferable to casually tossing out off-the-top-of-your-head suggestions. Be prepared to argue why your recommendations are more attractive than other courses of action that are open. You'll find the case preparation exercises on Case-TUTOR helpful in performing this step, too.

Table 1

Key Financial Ratios: How to Calculate Them and What They Mean

Ratio	How Calculated	What It Shows
Profitability ratios		
1. Gross profit margin	$\dfrac{\text{Sales} - \text{Cost of goods sold}}{\text{Sales}}$	Shows the percentage of revenues available to cover operating expenses and yield a profit. Higher is better and the trend should be upward.
2. Operating profit margin (or return on sales)	$\dfrac{\text{Sales} - \text{Operating expenses}}{\text{Sales}}$ or $\dfrac{\text{Operating income}}{\text{Sales}}$	Shows the profitability of current operations without regard to interest charges and income taxes. Higher is better and the trend should be upward.
3. Net profit margin (or net return on sales)	$\dfrac{\text{Profits after taxes}}{\text{Sales}}$	Shows after tax profits per dollar of sales. Higher is better and the trend should be upward.
4. Return on total assets	$\dfrac{\text{Profits after taxes} + \text{interest}}{\text{Total assets}}$	A measure of the return on total investment in the enterprise. Interest is added to after tax profits to form the numerator since total assets are financed by creditors as well as by stockholders. Higher is better and the trend should be upward.
5. Return on stockholders' equity	$\dfrac{\text{Profits after taxes}}{\text{Total stockholders' equity}}$	Shows the return stockholders are earning on their investment in the enterprise. A return in the 12-15% range is "average", and the trend should be upward.
6. Earnings per share	$\dfrac{\text{Profits after taxes}}{\text{Number of shares of common stock outstanding}}$	Shows the earnings for each share of common stock outstanding. The trend should be upward, and the bigger the annual percentage gains, the better.
Liquidity Ratios		
1. Current ratio	$\dfrac{\text{Current assets}}{\text{Current liabilities}}$	Shows a firm's ability to pay current liabilities using assets that can be converted to cash in the near term. Ratio should definitely be higher than 1.0; ratios of 2 or higher are better still.
2. Quick ratio (or acid-test ratio)	$\dfrac{\text{Current assets} - \text{Inventory}}{\text{Current liabilities}}$	Shows a firm's ability to pay current liabilities without relying on the sale of its inventories.

Table 1 *continued*

3. Working capital	Current assets – current liabilities	Bigger amounts are better because the company has more internal funds available to (1) pay its current liabilities on a timely basis and (2) finance inventory expansion, additional accounts receivable, and a larger base of operations without resorting to borrowing or raising more equity capital.
Leverage Ratios		
1. Debt-to-assets ratio	$\dfrac{\text{Total debt}}{\text{Total assets}}$	Measures the extent to which borrowed funds have been used to finance the firm's operations. Low fractions or ratios are better—high fractions indicate overuse of debt and greater risk of bankruptcy.
2. Debt-to-equity ratio	$\dfrac{\text{Total debt}}{\text{Total stockholders' equity}}$	Should usually be less than 1.0. High ratios (especially above 1.0) signal excessive debt, lower creditworthiness, and weaker balance sheet strength.
3. Long-term debt-to-equity ratio	$\dfrac{\text{Long-term debt}}{\text{Total stockholders' equity}}$	Shows the balance between debt and equity in the firm's *long-term* capital structure. Low ratios indicate greater capacity to borrow additional funds if needed.
4. Times-interest-earned (or coverage) ratio	$\dfrac{\text{Operating income}}{\text{Interest expenses}}$	Measures the ability to pay annual interest charges. Lenders usually insist on a minimum ratio of 2.0, but ratios above 3.0 signal better creditworthiness.
Activity Ratios		
1. Days of inventory	$\dfrac{\text{Sales} \div 365}{\text{Inventory}}$	Measures inventory management efficiency. Fewer days of inventory are usually better.
2. Inventory turnover	$\dfrac{\text{Sales}}{\text{Inventory}}$	Measures the number of inventory turns per year. Higher is better.
3. Average collection period	$\dfrac{\text{Accounts receivable}}{\text{Total sales} \div 365}$ or $\dfrac{\text{Accounts receivable}}{\text{Average daily sales}}$	Indicates the average length of time the firm must wait after making a sale to receive cash payment. A shorter collection time is better.
Other Important Measures of Financial Performance		
1. Dividend yield on common stock	$\dfrac{\text{Annual dividends per share}}{\text{Current market price per share}}$	A measure of the return that shareholders receive in the form of dividends. A "typical" dividend yield is 2-3%. The dividend yield for fast-growth companies is often below 1% (maybe even 0); the dividend yield for slow-growth companies can run 4-5%.
2. Price-earnings ratio	$\dfrac{\text{Current market price per share}}{\text{Earnings per share}}$	P-e ratios above 20 indicate strong investor confidence in a firm's outlook and earnings growth; firms whose future earnings are at risk or likely to grow slowly typically have ratios below 12.
3. Dividend payout ratio	$\dfrac{\text{Annual dividends per share}}{\text{Earnings per share}}$	Indicates the percentage of after-tax profits paid out as dividends.
4. Internal cash flow	After tax profits + Depreciation	A quick and rough estimate of the cash a company's business is generating after payment of operating expenses, interest, and taxes. Such amounts can be used for dividend payments or funding capital expenditures.

As long as you are conscientious in preparing your analysis and recommendations, and have ample reasons, evidence, and arguments to support your views, you shouldn't fret unduly about whether what you've prepared is "the right answer" to the case. In case analysis there is rarely just one right approach or set of recommendations. Managing companies and crafting and executing strategies are not such exact sciences that there exists a single provably correct analysis and action plan for each strategic situation. Of course, some analyses and action plans are better than others; but, in truth, there's nearly always more than one good way to analyze a situation and more than one good plan of action. So, if you have carefully prepared the case by either completing one of the Case-TUTOR case preparation exercises or developing your own answers to the assignment questions for the case, don't lose confidence in the correctness of your work and judgment.

Participating in Class Discussion of a Case

Classroom discussions of cases are sharply different from attending a lecture class. In a case class students do most of the talking. The instructor's role is to solicit student participation, keep the discussion on track, ask "Why?" often, offer alternative views, play the devil's advocate (if no students jump in to offer opposing views), and otherwise lead the discussion. The students in the class carry the burden for analyzing the situation and for being prepared to present and defend their diagnoses and recommendations. Expect a classroom environment, therefore, that calls for *your* size-up of the situation, *your* analysis, what actions *you* would take, and why *you* would take them. Do not be dismayed if, as the class discussion unfolds, some insightful things are said by your fellow classmates that you did not think of. It is normal for views and analyses to differ and for the comments of others in the class to expand your own thinking about the case. As the old adage goes, "Two heads are better than one." So it is to be expected that the class as a whole will do a more penetrating and searching job of case analysis than will any one person working alone. This is the power of group effort, and its virtues are that it will help you see more analytical applications, let you test your analyses and judgments against those of your peers, and force you to wrestle with differences of opinion and approaches.

To orient you to the classroom environment on the days a case discussion is scheduled, we compiled the following list of things to expect:

1. *Expect the instructor to assume the role of extensive questioner and listener.*

2. *Expect students to do most of the talking. The case method enlists a maximum of individual participa– tion in class discussion. It is not enough to be present as a silent observer; if every student took this approach, there would be no discussion. (Thus, expect a portion of your grade to be based on your participation in case discussions.)*

3. *Be prepared for the instructor to probe for reasons and supporting analysis.*

4. *Expect and tolerate challenges to the views expressed. All students have to be willing to submit their conclusions for scrutiny and rebuttal. Each student needs to learn to state his or her views without fear of disapproval and to overcome the hesitation of speaking out. Learning respect for the views and approaches of others is an integral part of case analysis exercises. But there are times when it is OK to swim against the tide of majority opinion. In the practice of management, there is always room for originality and unorthodox approaches. So while discussion of a case is a group process, there is no compulsion for you or anyone else to cave in and conform to group opinions and group consensus.*

5. *Don't be surprised if you change your mind about some things as the discussion unfolds. Be alert to how these changes affect your analysis and recommendations (in the event you get called on).*

6. *Expect to learn a lot in class as the discussion of a case progresses; furthermore, you will find that the cases build on one another—what you learn in one case helps prepare you for the next case discussion.*

There are several things you can do on your own to be good and look good as a participant in class discussions:

Although you should do your own independent work and independent thinking, don't hesitate before (and after) class to discuss the case with other students. In real life, managers often discuss the company's problems and situation with other people to refine their own thinking.

- *In participating in the discussion, make a conscious effort to contribute, rather than just talk. There is a big difference between saying something that builds the discussion and offering a long-winded, off-the-cuff remark that leaves the class wondering what the point was.*

- *Avoid the use of "I think," "I believe," and "I feel"; instead, say, "My analysis shows —" and "The company should do _____.because _____." Always give supporting reasons and evidence for your views; then your instructor won't have to ask you "Why?" every time you make a comment.*

- *In making your points, assume that everyone has read the case and knows what it says; avoid reciting and rehashing information in the case—instead, use the data and information to explain your assessment of the situation and to support your position.*

- Bring the printouts of the work you've done on Case-Tutor or the notes you've prepared (usually two or three pages' worth) to class and rely on them extensively when you speak. There's no way you can remember everything off the top of your head—especially the results of your number crunching. To reel off the numbers or to present all five reasons why, instead of one, you will need good notes. When you have prepared thoughtful answers to the study questions and use them as the basis for your comments, *everybody* in the room will know you are well prepared, and your contribution to the case discussion will stand out.

Preparing a Written Case Analysis

Preparing a written case analysis is much like preparing a case for class discussion, except that your analysis must be more complete and put in report form. Unfortunately, though, there is no ironclad procedure for doing a written case analysis. All we can offer are some general guidelines and words of wisdom—this is because company situations and management problems are so diverse that no one mechanical way to approach a written case assignment always works.

Your instructor may assign you a specific topic around which to prepare your written report. Or, alternatively, you may be asked to do a comprehensive written case analysis, where the expectation is that you will (1) *identify* all the pertinent issues that management needs to address, (2) perform whatever *analysis* and *evaluation* is appropriate, and (3) propose an *action plan* and *set of recommendations* addressing the issues you have identified. In going through the exercise of identify, evaluate, and recommend, keep the following pointers in mind.[3]

Identification   It is essential early on in your paper that you provide a sharply focused diagnosis of strategic issues and key problems and that you demonstrate a good grasp of the company's present situation. Make sure you can identify the firm's strategy (use the concepts and tools in Chapters 1–8 as diagnostic aids) and that you can pinpoint whatever strategy implementation issues may exist (again, consult the material in Chapters 9–11 for diagnostic help). Consult the key points we have provided at the end of each chapter for further diagnostic suggestions. Review the study questions for the case on Case-Tutor. Consider beginning your paper with an overview of the company's situation, its strategy, and the significant problems and issues that confront management. State problems/issues as clearly and precisely as you can. Unless it is necessary to do so for emphasis, avoid recounting facts and history about the company (assume your professor has read the case and is familiar with the organization).

Analysis and Evaluation This is usually the hardest part of the report. Analysis is hard work! Check out the firm's financial ratios, its profit margins and rates of return, and its capital structure, and decide how strong the firm is financially. Table 1 contains a summary of various financial ratios and how they are calculated. Use it to assist in your financial diagnosis. Similarly, look at marketing, production, managerial competence, and other factors underlying the organization's strategic successes and failures. Decide whether the firm has valuable resource strengths and competencies and, if so, whether it is capitalizing on them.

Check to see if the firm's strategy is producing satisfactory results and determine the reasons why or why not. Probe the nature and strength of the competitive forces confronting the company. Decide whether and why the firm's competitive position is getting stronger or weaker. Use the tools and concepts you have learned about to perform whatever analysis and evaluation is appropriate. Work through the case preparation exercise on Case-Tutor if one is available for the case you've been assigned.

In writing your analysis and evaluation, bear in mind four things:

1. *You are obliged to offer analysis and evidence to back up your conclusions. Do not rely on unsupported opinions, over-generalizations, and platitudes as a substitute for tight, logical argument backed up with facts and figures.*

2. *If your analysis involves some important quantitative calculations, use tables and charts to present the calculations clearly and efficiently. Don't just tack the exhibits on at the end of your report and let the reader figure out what they mean and why they were included. Instead, in the body of your report cite some of the key numbers, highlight the conclusions to be drawn from the exhibits, and refer the reader to your charts and exhibits for more details.*

3. *Demonstrate that you have command of the strategic concepts and analytical tools to which you have been exposed. Use them in your report.*

4. *Your interpretation of the evidence should be reasonable and objective. Be wary of preparing a one-sided argument that omits all aspects not favorable to your conclusions. Likewise, try not to exaggerate or overdramatize. Endeavor to inject balance into your analysis and to avoid emotional rhetoric. Strike phrases such as "I think," "I feel," and "I believe" when you edit your first draft and write in "My analysis shows," instead.*

Recommendations The final section of the written case analysis should consist of a set of definite recommendations and a plan of action. Your set of recommendations should address all of the problems/ issues you identified and analyzed. If the recommendations come as a surprise or do not follow logically from the analysis, the effect is to weaken greatly your suggestions of what to do. Obviously, your recommendations for actions should offer a reasonable prospect of success. High-risk, bet-the-company recommendations should be made with caution. State how your recommendations will solve the problems you identified. Be sure the company is financially able to carry out what you recommend; also check to see if your recommendations are workable in terms of acceptance by the persons involved, the organization's competence to implement them, and prevailing market and environmental constraints. Try not to hedge or weasel on the actions you believe should be taken.

By all means state your recommendations in sufficient detail to be meaningful—get down to some definite nitty-gritty specifics. Avoid such unhelpful statements as "the organization should do more planning" or "the company should be more aggressive in marketing its product." For instance, if you determine that "the firm should improve its market position," then you need to set forth exactly how you think this should be done. Offer a definite agenda for action, stipulating a timetable and sequence for initiating actions, indicating priorities, and suggesting who should be responsible for doing what.

In proposing an action plan, remember there is a great deal of difference between, on the one hand, being responsible for a decision that may be costly if it proves in error and, on the other hand, casually suggesting courses of action that might be taken when you do not have to bear the responsibility for any of the consequences. A good rule to follow in making your recommendations is: *Avoid recommending anything you would not yourself be willing to do if you were in management's shoes.* The importance of learning to develop good managerial judgment is indicated by the fact that, even though the same information and operating data may be available to every manager or executive in an organization, the quality of the judgments about what the information means and which actions need to be taken does vary from person to person.[4]

It goes without saying that your report should be well organized and well written. Great ideas amount to little unless others can be convinced of their merit—this takes tight logic, the presentation of convincing evidence, and persuasively written arguments.

Preparing an Oral Presentation

During the course of your business career it is very likely that you will be called upon to prepare and give a number of oral presentations. For this reason, it is common in courses of this nature to assign cases for oral presentation to the whole class. Such assignments give you an opportunity to hone your presentation skills.

The preparation of an oral presentation has much in common with that of a written case analysis. Both require identification of the strategic issues and problems confronting the company, analysis of industry conditions and the company's situation, and the development of a thorough, well-thought out action plan. The substance of your analysis and quality of your recommendations in an oral presentation should be no different than in a written report. As with a written assignment, you'll need to demonstrate command of the relevant strategic concepts and tools of analysis and your recommendations should contain sufficient detail to provide clear direction for management. The main difference between an oral presentation and a written case is in the delivery format. Oral presentations rely principally on verbalizing your diagnosis, analysis, and recommendations and visually enhancing and supporting your oral discussion with colorful, snappy slides (usually created on Microsoft's PowerPoint software).

Typically, oral presentations involve group assignments. Your instructor will provide the details of the assignment—how work should be delegated among the group members and how the presentation should be conducted. Some instructors prefer that presentations begin with issue identification, followed by analysis of the industry and company situation analysis, and conclude with a recommended action plan to improve company performance. Other instructors prefer that the presenters assume that the class has a good understanding of the external industry environment and the company's competitive position and expect the presentation to be strongly focused on the group's recommended action plan and supporting analysis and arguments. The latter approach requires cutting straight to the heart of the case and supporting each recommendation with detailed analysis and persuasive reasoning. Still other instructors may give you the latitude to structure your presentation however you and your group members see fit.

Regardless of the style preferred by your instructor, you should take great care in preparing for the presentation. A good set of slides with good content and good visual appeal is essential to a first-rate presentation. Take some care to choose a nice slide design, font size and style, and color scheme. We suggest including slides covering each of the following areas:

- An opening slide covering the "title" of the presentation and names of the presenters.
- A slide showing an outline of the presentation (perhaps with presenters' names by each topic).
- One or more slides showing the key problems and strategic issues that management needs to address.
- A series of slides covering your analysis of the company's situation.
- A series of slides containing your recommendations and the supporting arguments and reasoning for each recommendation—one slide for each recommendation and the associated reasoning has a lot of merit.

You and your team members should carefully plan and rehearse your slide show to maximize impact and minimize distractions. The slide show should include all of the pizzazz necessary to garner the attention of the audience, but not so much that it distracts from the content of what group members are saying to the class. You should remember that the role of slides is to help you communicate your points to the audience. Too many graphics, images, colors, and transitions may divert the audience's attention from what is being said or disrupt the flow of the presentation. Keep in mind that visually dazzling slides rarely hide a shallow or superficial or otherwise flawed case analysis from a perceptive audience. Most instructors will tell you that first-rate slides will definitely enhance a well-delivered presentation but that impressive visual aids, if accompanied by weak analysis and poor oral delivery, still adds up to a substandard presentation.

Researching Companies and Industries via the Internet and Online Data Services

Very likely, there will be occasions when you need to get additional information about some of the assigned cases, perhaps because your instructor has asked you to do further research on the industry or company or because you are simply curious about what has happened to the company since the case was written. These days it is relatively easy to run down recent industry developments and to find out whether a company's strategic and financial situation has improved, deteriorated, or changed little since the conclusion of the case. The amount of information about companies and industries available on the Internet and through online data services is formidable and expanding rapidly.

It is a fairly simple matter to go to company Web sites, click on the investor information offerings and press release files, and get quickly to useful information. Most company Web sites allow you to view or print the company's quarterly and annual reports, its 10K and 10Q filings with the Securities and Exchange Commission, and various company press releases of interest. Frequently, a company's Web site will also provide information about its mission and vision statements, values statements, codes of ethics, and strategy information, as well as charts of the company's stock price. The company's recent press releases typically contain reliable information about what of interest has been going on—new product introductions, recent alliances and partnership agreements, recent acquisitions, summaries of the latest financial results, tidbits about the company's strategy, guidance about future revenues and earnings, and other late-breaking company developments. Some company Web pages also include links to the home pages of industry trade associations where you can find information about industry size, growth, recent industry news, statistical trends, and future outlook. Thus, an early step in researching a company on the Internet is always to go to its Web site and see what's available.

Online Data Services

Lexis-Nexis, Bloomberg Financial News Services, and other on-line subscription services available in many university libraries provide access to a wide array of business reference material. For example, the web-based Lexis-Nexis Academic Universe contains business news articles from general news sources, business publications, and industry trade publications. Broadcast transcripts from financial news programs are also available through Lexis-Nexis, as are full-text 10-Ks, 10-Qs, annual reports, and company profiles for more than 11,000 U.S. and international companies. Your business librarian should be able to direct you to the resources available through your library that will aid you in your research.

Public and Subscription Websites with Good Information

Plainly, you can use a search engine such as Google or Yahoo! or MSN to find the latest news on a company or articles written by reporters that have appeared in the business media. These can be very valuable in running down information about recent company developments. However, keep in mind that the information retrieved by a search engine is "unfiltered" and may include sources that are not reliable or that contain inaccurate or misleading information. Be wary of information provided by authors who are unaffiliated with reputable organizations or publications and articles that were published in off-beat sources or on Web sites with an agenda. Be especially careful in relying on the accuracy of information you find posted on various bulletin boards. Articles covering a company or issue should be copyrighted or published by a reputable source. If you are turning in a paper containing information gathered from the Internet, you should cite your sources (providing the Internet address and date visited); it is also wise to print Web pages for your research file (some Web pages are updated frequently).

The Wall Street Journal, Business Week, Forbes, Barron's, and *Fortune* are all good sources of articles on companies. *The Wall Street Journal Interactive Edition* contains the same information that is available daily in its print version of the paper, but also maintains a searchable database of all *Wall Street Journal* articles published during the past few years. *Fortune* and *Business Week* also make the content of the most current issue available online to subscribers as well as provide archives sections that allow you to search for articles related to a particular keyword that were published during the past few years.

The following Websites are particularly good locations for company and industry information:

Securities and Exchange Commission EDGAR database (contains company 10-Ks, 10-Qs, etc.)	http://www.sec.gov/cgi-bin/srch-edgar
CNN Money	http://money.cnn.com
Hoover's Online	http://hoovers.com
The Wall Street Journal Interactive Edition	http://www.wsj.com
Business Week	http://www.businessweek.com
Fortune	http://www.fortune.com
MSN Money Central	http://moneycentral.msn.com
Yahoo! Finance	http://finance.yahoo.com/

Some of these Internet sources require subscriptions in order to access their entire databases.

Learning Comes Quickly   With a modest investment of time, you will learn how to use Internet sources and search engines to run down information on companies and industries quickly and efficiently. And it is a skill that will serve you well into the future. Once you become familiar with the data available at the different Web sites mentioned above and with using a search engine, you will know where to go to look for the particular information that you want. Search engines nearly always turn up too many information sources that match your request rather than two few; the trick is to learn to zero in on those most relevant to what you are looking for. Like most things, once you get a little experience under your belt on how to do company and industry research on the Internet, you will find that you can readily find the information you need.

The Ten Commandments of Case Analysis

As a way of summarizing our suggestions about how to approach the task of case analysis, we have compiled what we like to call "The Ten Commandments of Case Analysis." They are shown in Table 2. If you observe all or even most of these commandments faithfully as you prepare a case either for class discussion or for a written report, your chances of doing a good job on the assigned cases will be much improved. Hang in there, give it your best shot, and have some fun exploring what the real world of strategic management is all about.

Table 2

The Ten Commandments of Case Analysis

To be observed in written reports and oral presentations, and while participating in class discussions.

1. Go through the case twice, once for a quick overview and once to gain full command of the facts; then take care to explore the information in every one of the case exhibits.

2. Make a complete list of the problems and issues that the company's management needs to address.

3. Be thorough in your analysis of the company's situation (either work through the case preparation exercises on Case-TUTOR or make a minimum of 1 to 2 pages of notes detailing your diagnosis).

4. Look for opportunities to apply the concepts and analytical tools in the text chapters—all of the cases in the book have very definite ties to the material in one or more of the text chapters!!!!

5. Do enough number crunching to discover the story told by the data presented in the case. (To help you comply with this commandment, consult Table 1 in this section to guide your probing of a company's financial condition and financial performance.)

6. Support any and all off-the-cuff opinions with well-reasoned arguments and numerical evidence; don't stop until you can purge "I think" and "I feel" from your assessment and, instead, are able to rely completely on "My analysis shows."

7. Prioritize your recommendations and make sure they can be carried out in an acceptable time frame with the available resources.

8. Support each recommendation with persuasive argument and reasons as to why it makes sense and should result in improved company performance.

9. Review your recommended action plan to see if it addresses all of the problems and issues you identified—any set of recommendations that does not address all of the issues and problems you identified is incomplete and insufficient.

10. Avoid recommending any course of action that could have disastrous consequences if it doesn't work out as planned; therefore, be as alert to the downside risks of your recommendations as you are to their upside potential and appeal.

Endnotes

[1] Charles I. Gragg, "Because Wisdom Can't Be Told," in *The Case Method at the Harvard Business School*, ed. M. P. McNair (New York: McGraw-Hill, 1954), p. 11.

[2] Ibid., pp. 12–14; and D. R. Schoen and Philip A. Sprague, "What Is the Case Method?" in *The Case Method at the Harvard Business School*, ed. M. P. McNair, pp. 78–79.

[3] For some additional ideas and viewpoints, you may wish to consult Thomas J. Raymond, "Written Analysis of Cases," in *The Case Method at the Harvard Business School*, ed. M. P. McNair, pp. 139–63. Raymond's article includes an actual case, a sample analysis of the case, and a sample of a student's written report on the case.

[4] Gragg, "Because Wisdom Can't Be Told," p. 10.

Richard Ivey School of Business
The University of Western Ontario

9B08M057

The Piercer

"Don't forget, your business idea pitch is due in two weeks," said Professor Sharen at the end of class. Jessica Pierce turned to look at her project team mate, Ashley Mound. Jessica and Ashley were fourth-year management and organizational studies students at Brescia University College, taking an introduction to entrepreneurship course.

Ashley and Jessica had developed an idea for the assignment: a personal safety alarm that both shrieked and flashed lights when the person carrying it set off the alarm function. Given the concern that many people had over personal safety, it seemed like a great business idea.

In order to present their idea, they needed to show that there was a market for this product and that they had a way to sell it to consumers. The problem was that they did not really know how or where to start to get the information that they needed. They had a lot of work to do to be ready to present their project in the next two weeks.

THE ASSIGNMENT

The business pitch assignment was challenging. Sharen had asked students to develop an interesting business idea and present it to a panel of potential investors. These investors included a successful serial entrepreneur, a business consultant who practised in the area of small- and medium-size enterprises, an owner of a marketing and advertising services business and a business professor.

The students were asked to present an innovative idea, show why it would be successful in the market place, demonstrate potential markets, show the business model and sell themselves to the investors as entrepreneurs.

The investors were instructed to view their investments as seed money to enable the students to further develop business plans and prototypes of their ideas. The students weren't required to complete a financial analysis for this assignment.

The investors were asked to assess project ideas on the basis of the feasibility of the idea and whether they believed that the entrepreneurs would be able to deliver. They could consider the appeal of the idea itself, the logistics and operations required to run the business, the effectiveness of the business plan, the long-term viability of the business or the size of the market.

The assignment would be graded 50 per cent based on how much money the teams received from the investors and 50 per cent on the quality of their presentation by the professor.

THE IDEA

The Piercer was a small device that hung on a chain worn around the neck. When activated, The Piercer emitted a piercing sound that traveled for approximately 500 meters, as well as a bright flashing light. To deactivate The Piercer, the wearer had to push two buttons simultaneously. This was to prevent an attacker from being able to deactivate the device.

The piercing noise and the bright flashing light were designed to scare away attackers and attract those who might assist the person being attacked. In the situation of imminent attack, a person would not have to rely on their voice or bring a whistle to their mouth to signal for help.

Ashley and Jessica had researched costs and thought that by manufacturing in China, they could make The Piercer for $2 and sell it for $7.50 wholesale, with a retail price of $14.95.

The idea made sense to Ashley and Jessica. It fit with recent social and demographic trends as aging baby boomers began to need assistance with injuries and falls, and with increased general concerns about health, safety and violence.

WHAT NEXT?

Jessica and Ashley thought that they had a good idea. Now they had to prove it. What were the target markets for this product? How big were they? Which ones should they choose? How should they sell to them? What proportion of the target market should they expect to capture? Where should they look for information to help them make these decisions?

A SIMPLE GUIDE TO INFORMATION RESOURCES AND EVALUATION

Ashley and Jessica must do secondary research to be able to evaluate and implement their idea. They will need to consider 1) how to evaluate resources, 2) how to develop effective search strategies and 3) how to identify proprietary resources that support the case for this business.

1. How to Evaluate Resources

Information is available everywhere, and for this reason, Jessica and Ashley need to be able to discriminate between good and poor quality information. Appropriate information usage for an academic project includes evaluating and assessing resources for reliability and credibility.

Goals

- Ashley and Jessica should be able to locate and differentiate free versus proprietary web resources.
- They should be able to identify a quality website.
- They should be able to evaluate books and other print resources for quality and reliability.
- They should understand the difference between scholarly and non-scholarly articles and resources.
- They should be able to cite information properly.

Free Versus Proprietary Web Resources

Many students think that the World Wide Web has the answers for everything. While the web can have valuable information, students pay (through their tuition) to have access to quality proprietary information resources.

Ashley and Jessica could examine some free web sites to help them. For example, associations, company information and government information can be very helpful, as long as the user knows how to determine the quality of a website.

Quality Web Sites

Anyone anywhere can make a website. Just because it is on the web, does not mean it is good quality or reliable. When Ashley and Jessica are evaluating websites, they need to consider:

Who is providing the information?
- Is it a government institution, a university or a company?
- Does the url make sense (e.g. .org, .edu, .on.ca)?
- Does the owner of the website have anything to gain by providing the information?
- Does the owner of the website have good credentials?
- Has anyone updated the website recently?

Note that Wikipedia is not necessarily a reliable resource. Anyone anywhere can modify these pages. While it might be a place to find some resources or links, students should not cite Wikipedia as a reliable resource in an academic paper.

The University of Alberta put together a good web evaluation checklist:

http://www.library.ualberta.ca/instruction/science/evalweb.pdf

For a more comprehensive list on evaluating web resources, see the bibliography on the topic:

http://www.lib.vt.edu/help/instruct/evaluate/evalbiblio.html

Evaluating Other Resources

Ashley and Jessica need to be critical of all the resources they use, not just websites. Ideally, they should be able to discriminate between proprietary and non-proprietary websites, scholarly and non-scholarly resources and evaluate the quality of any book used.

Things for Ashley and Jessica to consider include:
- Who published the book or made the information available?
- How old is the information?
- Has the information been updated recently?
- Is the information peer reviewed? Does this matter?
- Did the library buy and recommend the resource?
- Is the author credible?

Scholarly Versus Non-Scholarly Resources

An academic library will provide access to both scholarly and non-scholarly resources. Scholarly work generally refers to published work that has been through a peer review process. Especially in the field of business, there are many practitioner resources. Therefore, Jessica and Ashley need to be aware of the type of information they are gathering. For example, industry trends, say from Standard and Poors NetAdvantage, is not a scholarly resource, yet the information within them could be valuable. Alternatively, ProQuest ABI Inform Global provides access to scholarly articles.

Ashley and Jessica may also consider the relative value of evidence or fact versus opinion. Students should not read things and trust that what they are reading is accurate. Students should think about the rigor with which the argument is made and the evidence presented.
- Is there evidence to back up a claim?
- Has the evidence been collected in a reliable way?
- Is the author stating an opinion without backing up his or her ideas?

Citing Work

It is important that Ashley and Jessica cited their work properly, to avoid accidental plagiarism.

Some of the more confusing things to cite include Statistics Canada data or online information. Statistics Canada has a website that describes systematically how to cite its tables, publications or other datasets:

http://www.statcan.ca/english/freepub/12-591-XIE/12-591-XIE2006001.htm

In addition, most academic libraries will have information about citation procedures, or will have copies of publication manuals available for borrowing. Any librarian can be asked about citation procedures.

2. How to Develop Search Strategies

Goals

- Ashley and Jessica should know the difference between searching in different search fields, such as the abstract field and title field
- They should be able to use this technology to search the unique fields
- They should be able to use the "AND," "OR," or "NOT" features of a search engine to help narrow their search.
- They should understand what truncation and proximity search strategies are, and how that influences a search.

Most search engines that index information have similar features. If Ashley and Jessica understand the concepts in searching, they can apply them to any search engine.

Take Advantage of Search Fields

For example, records in an index have many different fields such as keywords, title, author, publication title, document title, abstract, full document, date, author, etc. It is often possible to specify what part of the record to search in, which helps to be more specific with the search. Searching an entire text document may retrieve less meaningful records than a search of just abstracts.

Use Boolean Search Strategies

Using "AND" and "OR" can be helpful in expanding or narrowing a search. AND narrows a search and OR expands it. Using the term "NOT" can also be helpful, but should be limited. For example, searching for beer companies will retrieve companies on diamonds (DeBeers). Excluding the term "diamond" from a search on beer companies could be helpful in narrowing one's search.

Truncation and Proximity

Many search engines allow for truncation and proximity searching. In ProQuest, an asterisk symbol will truncate. For example, if one types "leader*" into a search box, records with leader, leaders and leadership will be retrieved. This helps capture all variations of a word.

Proximity searching refers to how close two words are together in a document. Presumably, if two words are close together in a document, they are more likely to have something to do with each other. In ProQuest, a "w/1" or "w/2" ("w/3," etc.) facilitates proximity searching. For example, if Ashley or Jessica typed "organizational w/3 learning" in the search box, they will retrieve documents where the word "organizational" is within three words of "learning."

Find Creative Ways In

There are many different ways to find information. Knowing a company name or a competitor's name is convenient. Taking advantage of key words (or subject terms) also is a good way to search.

It is also a good idea to brainstorm for synonyms prior to beginning a search. Being deliberate about a search strategy and deciding on what concepts to combine can really help make the search go easier.

Searching is iterative as well. One is advised to read some articles to learn the jargon of the topic, then go back and do the search again using the subject jargon. Most librarians will help on developing a search strategy!

3. How to Identify Proprietary Resources

Goals

Ashley and Jessica should be able to identify library resources and understand what type of information they can find in various types of resources.

The following databases are some of the library databases that Ashley and Jessica could consider. They could also go to the library (or call or e-mail) and ask for assistance. Library staff will know what resources the library has, if there are any other resources that may be of use and how to access and use the resources.

Finding Background Scholarly Articles

ProQuest ABI Inform Global is a database that indexes business and management journal articles. Most of the articles are available in full text, and both scholarly and non-scholarly articles are available. The search box in ProQuest has a drop-down menu on the right that allows users to search in specific fields. For example, users can search the title, abstract, author, company or publication fields.

Scopus is a database that indexes articles on the social sciences, life sciences, physical sciences and health sciences. For the purposes of a business or entrepreneurship project, searching only the social sciences category would be appropriate. This resource indexed scholarly articles.

Google Scholar is a free resource that indexes scholarly information from the World Wide Web. There is an advanced search engine feature to help specify a search. Many academic institutions integrate access to full text articles with Google Scholar. This means that any article the student has access to via the library, is also available to them via Google Scholar. Because Google Scholar is integrated with library resources, the student will likely need to either be on campus, or logged into the off-campus proxy server to take advantage of these services. If they are off campus or not logged into the proxy server the student can still search Google Scholar, but access to full text resources may be limited.

Finding News and Magazine Articles

Factiva is a database that indexes newspapers and magazines. While this resource does not index scholarly articles, it is a broad resource that captures current global news and events.

LexisNexis has a comprehensive database that indexes newspapers and magazines. There is also significant Canadian content indexed there.

Finding Industry Trends

Several databases including Standard & Poors NetAdvantage, Mintel and Marketline provide reports on industry trends. These databases provide regularly updated reports on broad industries. Each database tends to report on different industries, so students would have to do some trial and error research to find relevant reports. Students may find their topic is too narrow for these reports.

The Financial Post Investor Suite is a database that provides industry information from a Canadian perspective.

Finding Company Information

Company information may be important for a project such as The Piercer, especially for researching competitors.

MarketLine provides company information, including financial information, company descriptions and a list of competitors. Similarly, Hoovers provides comprehensive company descriptions. Not all companies are in both resources, therefore checking both resources is recommended for company research.

Marketing and Advertising

The World Advertising Research Center (WARC) is a resource that provides access to information about marketing and advertising, as well as to case studies of winning ad campaigns. Such a resource could be helpful in this context to see if other, similar products have been marketed, and if so, how they have been marketed. There is scholarly and non-scholarly information in this resource.

Technology Information

Both eMarketer and Forrester have information about technology trends. There may be information about the Internet, emerging technologies or electronic marketing.

Statistics and Demographics

Statistics Canada provides access to demographic data. Many secondary educational institutions participate in the Data Liberation Initiative. This means that information a member of the public would have to pay for, can be retrieved for free by a student. Students, through the academic library website, can use data for research. For more information about accessing statistics, students can talk to their subject librarian.

Some resources that Statistics Canada has that might be useful to find demographics include the *Market Research Handbook*, *Canadian Business Patterns*, CANSIM data, Census data, and *Canadian Social Trends*, among others.

There are other resources available via www.statcan.ca such as Community Profiles. Data are available down to groupings of the population of about 2,000 to 7,000 people, meaning students can find demographic data for each 2,000- to 7,000-person neighbourhood across the country.

Global Information

Although global research may not be as important for a product such as The Piercer, other entrepreneurial projects may require researching the global market. *Economic Intelligence Unit, Global Market Information Database* and *Business Monitor Online* are three resources that provide global market and industry information.

Other Helpful Resources

Students are encouraged to use the World Wide Web to help them find good information. For example, city homepages often have information about setting up a business. Association websites also can have helpful information. Also, banks have entrepreneurial information on their websites.

In addition, many books in the library explain how to develop small business plans or provide information on entrepreneurship.

Peter Green's First Day

Peter Green came home to his wife and new baby a dejected man. What a contrast to the morning, when he had left the apartment full of enthusiasm to tackle his first customer in his new job at Scott Carpets. And what a customer! Peabody Rug was the largest carpet retailer in the area and accounted for 15% of the entire volume of Peter's territory. When Peabody introduced a Scott product, other retailers were quick to follow with orders. So when Bob Franklin, the owner of Peabody Rug, had called District Manager John Murphy expressing interest in "Carpet Supreme", Scott's newest commercial duty home carpet, Peter knew that a $15,000–$20,000 order was a real probability, and no small show for his first sale. And it was important to do well at the start, for John Murphy had made no bones about his scorn for the new breed of salespeople at Scott Carpet.

Murphy was of the old school: in the business since his graduation from a local high school, he had fought his way through the stiffest retail competition in the nation to be District Manager of the area at age fifty-eight. Murphy knew his textiles, and he knew his competitors' textiles. He knew his customers, and he knew how well his competitors knew his customers. Formerly, when Scott Carpet had needed to fill a sales position, it had generally raided the competition for experienced personnel, put them on a straight commission, and thereby managed to increase sales and maintain its good reputation for service at the same time. When Murphy had been promoted eight years ago to the position of District Manager, he had passed on his sales territory to Harvey Katchorian, a sixty-year-old mill rep and son of an immigrant who had also spent his life in the carpet trade. Harvey had had no trouble keeping up his sales and had retired from the company the previous spring after 45 years of successful service in the industry. Peter, in turn, was to take over Harvey's accounts, and Peter knew that John Murphy was not sure that his original legacy to Harvey was being passed on to the best salesperson.

Peter was one of the new force of salespeople from Scott's Sales Management Program. In 1976 top management had created a training program to compensate for the industry's dearth of younger salespeople with long-term management potential. Peter, a college graduate, had entered Scott's five-month training program immediately after college and was the first graduate of the program to be assigned to John Murphy's district. Murphy had made it known to top management from the start that he did not think the training program could compensate for on-the-job experience, and he was clearly withholding optimism about Peter's prospects as a salesperson despite Peter's fine performance during the training program.

Peter had been surprised, therefore, when Murphy volunteered to accompany him on his first week of sales "to ease your transition into the territory." As they entered the office at Peabody

This case was prepared by Laura Nash, Post Doctoral Research Fellow in Business and Ethics, under the supervision of Professor John B. Matthews, as the basis for class discussion rather than to illustrate either effective or ineffective handling of an administrative situation.

1

Rug, Murphy had even seemed friendly and said reassuringly, "I think you'll get along with Bob. He's a great guy—knows the business and has been a good friend of mine for years."

Everything went smoothly. Bob liked the new line and appeared ready to place a large order with Peter the following week, but he indicated that he would require some "help on the freight costs" before committing himself definitely. Peter was puzzled and unfamiliar with the procedure, but Murphy quickly stepped in and assured Bob that Peter would be able to work something out.

After the meeting, on their way back to the Scott Carpets' district office, Peter asked Murphy about freight costs. Murphy sarcastically explained the procedure: because of its large volume, Peabody regularly "asked for a little help to cover shipping costs," and got it from all or most suppliers. Bob Franklin was simply issued a credit for defective merchandise. By claiming he had received second-quality goods, Bob was entitled to a 10%–25% discount. The discount on defective merchandise had been calculated by the company to equal roughly the cost of shipping the 500 lb. rolls back to the mill, and so it just about covered Bob's own freight costs. The practice had been going on so long that Bob demanded "freight assistance" as a matter of course before placing a large order. Obviously, the merchandise was not defective, but by making an official claim, the sales representative could set in gear the defective merchandise compensation system. Murphy reiterated, as if to a two-year-old, the importance of a Peabody account to any sales rep, and shrugged off the freight assistance as part of doing business with such an influential firm.

Peter stared at Murphy. "Basically, what you're asking me to do, Mr. Murphy, is to lie to the front office." Murphy angrily replied, "Look, do you want to make it here or not? If you do, you ought to know you need Peabody's business. I don't know what kind of fancy thinking they taught you at college, but where I come from you don't call your boss a liar."

From the time he was a child, Peter Green had been taught not to lie or steal. He believed these principles were absolute and that one should support one's beliefs at whatever personal cost. But during college the only even remote test of his principles was his strict adherence to the honor system in taking exams.

As he reviewed the conversation with Murphy, it seemed to Peter that there was no way to avoid losing the Peabody account, which would look bad on his own record as well as Murphy's— not to mention the loss in commissions for them both. He felt badly about getting into a tiff with Murphy on his first day out in the territory, and knew Murphy would feel betrayed if one of his salespeople purposely lost a major account.

The only out he could see, aside from quitting, was to play down the whole episode. Murphy had not actually *ordered* Peter to submit a claim for damaged goods (was he covering himself legally?), so Peter could technically ignore the conversation and simply not authorize a discount. He knew very well, however, that such a course was only superficially passive, and that in Murphy's opinion he would have lost the account on purpose. As Peter sipped halfheartedly at a martini, he thought bitterly to himself, "Boy, they sure didn't prepare me for this in Management Training. And I don't even know if this kind of thing goes on in the rest of Murphy's district, let alone in Scott's 11 other districts."

2

THE FRAMEMAKERS

D. Wesley Balderson
University of Lethbridge

Robert and Teresa Norman faced a big decision. They were contemplating Robert leaving his job managing his father's painting business to set up their own retail picture-framing store. As they thought about this dilemma, their minds wandered back to the events that had led up to the impending decision. Robert had been raised in a small town about 20 miles south of Brandon, Manitoba. His father was a painter, and Robert had worked in the painting business part time for several years. Upon graduating from high school, he completed a two-year business administration in interior design course at a college in the United States. It was there that he met and married his wife, Teresa.

Teresa had studied interior design at college. She came from a small farming community near Robert's hometown. One of her favourite pastimes when she was growing up was taking pictures of the beautiful scenery and making frames for them. Teresa, an only child, had always been very independent. Her parents, farmers, spent a lot of time tending to the farm. Teresa started helping them when she was very young by doing the bookkeeping and other administrative jobs.

Although Robert had always thought he might come back to take over his father's painting business, he wanted to obtain some outside business experience first. As a result, he found a job in a Zellers store in Winnipeg after his graduation. Robert enjoyed working with people in the retail setting but felt frustrated working for a larger company. He wanted to be on his own and dreamed of someday running his own business. While Robert worked at Zellers, Teresa had been developing her photography skills, working for local retailers preparing catalogues. Though she was fairly busy with this, she did not feel as if she were being challenged.

Finally, after two years with Zellers, the Normans decided to leave Winnipeg and return to Brandon where they could begin to take over the painting business. Robert's father was pleased with their decision and, since he was approaching retirement age, allowed his son to assume a major role in the business. Norman managed the business for six years with Teresa doing the bookkeeping. But although it provided a steady income, he could see that the growth possibilities in terms of income and challenge were limited. In addition, he soon realized he didn't like painting as much as he thought he would. As a result, he and Teresa started looking around for sideline opportunities to earn a little extra money. One they particularly enjoyed was assembling and selling picture frames.

One day, while in Winnipeg to obtain some water-seal paint, Robert ran across a small retail store called U-Frame-It. He went in to look around and talk to the manager about the business. He was impressed by the manager's enthusiasm and noticed that the store was extremely busy. Robert immediately began wondering about the possibility of starting his own picture-framing store.

Excited by what he had seen, Robert returned to Brandon without even buying his paint and told Teresa what had happened. She was extremely enthusiastic about the idea. Robert's father was skeptical and, as Robert had expected, disappointed that they wanted to leave the family business.

Robert and Teresa needed to make their decision quickly. The manager of the U-Frame-It store had indicated that the franchise chain was looking at Brandon as a possible site for another outlet sometime in the future.

After a few days of evaluating their small business decision, Robert and Teresa Norman decided to open the picture-framing retail outlet in Brandon. Robert had learned a great deal about the business from his visit with the U-Frame-It franchise in Winnipeg. He convinced his father that the opportunity had promise. Both were aware that many people were now becoming do-it-yourselfers in home decorating.

His college training had taught Robert the importance of thorough investigation before starting a business. He realized he should do this even before deciding whether to start the business on his own or to become a franchisee. He contacted the Professional Picture Framers Association (PPFA) and learned that the average customer spends $32 per visit at a framing store. In checking framing costs with the U-Frame-It manager in Winnipeg, he confirmed this information. A typical per-customer profit statement for a framing shop was as follows:

Revenue	$32	(100%)
Materials	15	(47%)
Overhead (rent, utilities, wages, etc.)	9	(28%)
Profit per customer	8	(25%)

Robert knew there was one other framing store in Brandon, a city of 35,000. Using Winnipeg as an example, Robert calculated that a framing store could service a population of approximately 25,000 people and earn an acceptable profit.

While Robert was collecting his information, Teresa was conducting some of her own market research. She visited the only picture-framing store in Brandon and noted that the store was the busiest between the hours of 11 a.m. and 3 p.m. She also observed that many customers had some time to wait for available workstations and for the glue to dry. During this time, they browsed around the store looking at the merchandise.

Robert also attended an industry supplier seminar in Minneapolis. He was encouraged to learn that the do-it-yourself framing business was experiencing rapid growth throughout North America. While there, Robert learned about several picture-framing trade magazines and bought subscriptions for them. He also made valuable contacts with suppliers and other dealers.

Things looked more positive each day, so Robert closed down the painting business, and he and Teresa began preparing to open their new store, which they would call The Framemakers.

Robert and Teresa Norman immediately went to work organizing their new business. They had contemplated signing a franchise contract with U-Frame-It but decided against it when he found out he would have to pay a $20,000 franchise fee and royalties of 10 percent of sales just for the name and set-up assistance. In addition, the franchisor required that the stores follow a set format and that all supplies be purchased from them.

Robert's college training had taught him the importance of drawing up a business plan, so they prepared the following outline for their business:

- *Target market.* They thought the new store should cater to the price-conscious individual who wanted to save a few dollars by doing his or her own framing. What he had learned about the do-it-yourself market seemed particularly suitable for the new business. They judged that the target market was between the ages of 35 and 60 and could spend up to an hour in the store. This was based on their observations of the other framing store in Brandon.

- *Financial.* Based on data from the U-Frame-It franchise, Robert estimated start-up costs to be about $100,000. Since they were planning to lease space for the store, the capital requirements included only the purchase of shelves, fixtures, initial inventory, and tools. Because he and Teresa had $25,000 in equity to put into the venture, they expected to be able to borrow the remaining $75,000 from a local bank.

- *Personnel.* Robert and Teresa were hesitant to hire any employees until they were sure the business would be successful. In addition, they wanted to be totally involved in the business to better learn about all aspects of framing. The two would work full time, each doing whatever needed to be done.

- *Regulations.* They knew The Framemakers would need a business licence, which they would obtain from the city hall. They would operate the business as a proprietorship until the need to incorporate became evident.

- *Layout.* After looking at the U-Frame-It shop in Winnipeg, Robert drew up an interior layout plan he believed allowed efficiency and convenience for the store.

- *Location.* Although there weren't many available locations in Brandon, Robert recognized the need to locate in a high-traffic area of the city. This would not only be convenient for regular customers but, they hoped, would attract some walk-in customers as well.

After developing this business plan, Robert and Teresa began making contacts to get the business going. Within the next month, Robert was busy negotiating with suppliers, landlords, his banker, and the city hall to get the business started as soon as possible.

After selecting their location, Robert and Teresa Norman began securing merchandise for their initial inventory in earnest. They soon learned, however, that suppliers wanted to be paid before making deliveries. Therefore, Robert approached his local bank's manager to obtain the money he needed to get started. Although he had known his banker for a long time, he was surprised to find a less than positive reaction toward his proposal. Robert requested a $75,000 business loan, with he and Teresa contributing $25,000 of their own money to the estimated $100,000 cost of the venture.

The bank manager asked Robert to go home and prepare a detailed description of their needs, as well as a projected operating statement for the first year's operations. The Normans were upset by this negative reaction and decided to visit other banks to obtain the funds they needed. But they found out they would need to provide the requested information to obtain the money no matter where they went. Robert and Teresa spent two days working feverishly and came up with the statements shown in Figure 1.

Figure 1

The Framemakers
Financial Requirements, Year 1

Item	Amount	Source of Information
Inventory	$ 45,000	General estimate
Equipment and fixtures	35,000	Approximation
Opening promotion (trade show)	2,000	Price of booth
First month's rent	2,000	From landlord
Three months' salary (Robert and Teresa)	12,000	Estimated $4,000/month
First three months' advertising	3,600	One ad on TV and radio, and in newspaper
Miscellaneous	400	Estimate
Total	$100,000	

The Framemakers
Projected Income Statement, Year 1

	Per Customer (Professional Picture Framing Association Figures)		20 Customers a Day for 240 Days
Sales	$32	100%	$153,600
Expenses	24	75	115,200
Profit	8	25	38,400

When Robert took the proposals to the bank, the manager seemed impressed but still would not give approval for the loan. Some uncertainties about the statements still bothered the banker. Finally, after two weeks of collecting information—and pleading—the Normans' loan for $75,000 was approved. A major reason for the approval was their past dealings with the bank and their good credit standing. Now they could begin purchasing supplies to get started.

Before long, however, the Normans realized that they had underestimated many of their expenses. They learned, for example, that utilities, rent, and telephone all required initial deposits of $200. They also needed some additional supplies, even though they had overbought some unnecessary supplies from especially persistent salespeople. The landlord required the first and last months' rent before letting them move in. The equipment costs and inventory levels were higher than they had estimated. Finally, since the Normans had decided it would be better to incorporate their business, they faced additional legal costs for which they had not planned. The result of all these additions was that The Framemakers needed another $10,000—and the Normans hadn't even opened the doors!

Robert and Teresa didn't know what to do. They were hesitant to go back to the bank and ask for more money because of the difficulty they had had obtaining the first loan. However, they knew their chances of obtaining funding elsewhere were slim. On top of that, the time for the grand opening was rapidly approaching.

Questions

1. What aspects of Robert and Teresa Norman's backgrounds will contribute to their success with the picture-framing store?
2. What positive things have Robert and Teresa done in investigating the feasibility of the new store and what additional information might they have collected? From what sources could this information be obtained?
3. From the information provided, evaluate the business plan they have prepared for their new business.
4. Weigh the relevant pros and cons for the Normans of operating a U-Frame-It franchise instead of starting their business from scratch.
5. Evaluate the Normans' initial approach to obtaining financing for The Framemakers.
6. Assuming you are the banker, evaluate the financial requirements and projections Robert and Teresa prepared.

Richard Ivey School of Business
The University of Western Ontario

9B00M046

OHNO SWIM CLUB: ORGANIZATIONAL GOVERNANCE AND MISSION

Brian Welliver had mixed feelings as he drove to the board meeting with his wife, Linda. He was about to submit his resignation from the position of head coach of the swim club, OHNO. He was sad about not being with the children, who ranged from age six to 18, but he was somewhat happy about no longer having to deal with certain parents. As he drove, his mind wandered over the past three years and, most especially, the events of the past three months.

THREE YEARS AGO

OHNO was first created in conjunction with some parents who wished to be more involved in competitive swimming. OHNO was the initials of the three suburbs that this club was meant to service. This collection of suburbs made up a school district with several elementary and middle schools and two high schools. Welliver was self-employed, but also served part time as the head swim coach for one of those high schools. He saw a shortage of quality swimmers who tried out for his high school team, not for lack of enthusiasm, but because the students had little preparation. Other sports, such as basketball and baseball, did not have such a problem because of a very rich system of community-based programs, starting with very young children. For swimming, not much existed to prepare the participants for the level of physical conditioning and competition that they would face.

OHNO was created with the goal of introducing children in the three suburbs to competitive swimming before they reached the junior and senior high level. It was relatively low cost to avoid discouraging parents who might balk at paying fees for yet another organized children's sport. It also provided an off-season training opportunity for high-school swimmers. In addition, the spirit of the club was rather low key and encouraged individual accomplishments and improvement, rather than a focus on swim meet results. The club's goals were to introduce children to competitive swimming, develop their stamina, improve their techniques, while at the same time not "burn out" the children on the sport before they were old enough to compete at the junior and high school level. Welliver considered the burn-out factor to be very important because swimming is a sport that could be run all year round, unlike other sports such as baseball or soccer, where the weather and facilities automatically forced students to take a break.

In the greater metro area there were at least a dozen other swim clubs, many of whom had aggressive competitive missions, more stringent participation requirements and higher fees. OHNO was going after a market niche that these other clubs did not consider important and that was in a school district that could use the support.

The workouts were conducted in the district at various elementary and middle schools that had swimming pools. The children were divided into three groups, based on age and ability, and each group had at least one part-time coach. The school district was very generous in not demanding payment for pool rental until the club was mature enough to cover costs. This favor came from the fact that the club had a mission: in the long run, it would support the swimming programs at the two high schools. For the first three years, the club survived by the efforts of a dedicated group of parents, the deferment of pool fees and Welliver's sacrifices. Besides coaching, Welliver would do many of the backroom chores such as registration, scheduling competitive meets, negotiating fees and hiring young, certified coaches. In theory, he was to be paid a salary of $20,000 per year, but Welliver would frequently forego pay so that there would be sufficient cash to pay the other coaches.

After three years in operation, OHNO had approximately 90 regular swimmers and an annual revenue of about $50,000. It owed the district approximately $6,000 in back pool fees and owed Welliver about $2,000 in back pay. Financially, the club was becoming more stable and was starting to chip away at its back debts. A volunteer with a good heart, but no accounting background, took over the treasury function to lessen the time demands on Welliver. Unfortunately, this caused the books to get temporarily out of balance by almost $20,000.

THREE MONTHS AGO

At this point, several events were set into motion. Welliver knew he would need to replace the current coach for the beginning swimmers group in five months because the current coach was going to college. He was immediately informed that a member of the board might have found a replacement named Sveltlana. Sveltlana happened to be a woman who was a two-time member of the national Olympic team for an Eastern European country. A condition was made that she had to be hired almost immediately. Welliver had a hard time understanding why such a person would want to coach six-year-olds at a newly started, small swim club for $12 per hour. The board member who recommended her happened to be the president of a multimillion-dollar firm. His wife was a very active volunteer, and he had two young daughters in the program. When Welliver asked for details, he learned that Sveltlana needed to have an employment sponsor for visa purposes. She had some experience coaching high school kids, but not young children. The board member was willing to pay for the legal costs of getting the visa. He was also willing to donate $6,000 to subsidize her pay temporarily so she could be paid an extra $8 per hour above the club's regular pay of $12 per hour, for a total of $20 per hour. The donation was conditional upon the hiring of this specific coach, with no promise that additional donations would be made once the $6,000 was used up. It was strongly implied by the benefactor that, somehow, this coach should be used for the group in which his two daughters swam. In addition, if this coach was no longer employed by OHNO, then the balance of this donation was to be returned to the benefactor.

In a nutshell, Welliver was very concerned. First, it appeared that there could be potential legal liability with respect to hiring someone who was not a U.S. citizen. Second, this coach had to be hired immediately, rather than in five months. This would temporarily increase operating expenses, without causing an increase in revenue, at a time when the financial books were currently out of balance. Third, this coach was obviously not meant for the beginners. Therefore, a beginner's coach would have to be hired in five months anyway. Fourth, this coach would be paid more than all the other coaches, resulting in potential morale problems. Fifth, there was no guaranteed financing source that would exist after the $6,000 was used up. Sixth, it appeared that this kind of hiring would start moving the club away from its original mission. Last, it felt uncomfortable for such a young, small club to be financially beholden to one family. He had to admit his irritation that coaching decisions no longer appeared to be his sole domain.

In the course of two board meetings, Sveltlana was hired. Welliver realized that the majority of the board was made up of parents who lived outside the school district that this club was intended to serve. They were very active volunteers to be sure, but in retrospect it seemed odd that they had not joined any of the other swim clubs that served the metro area. They were very enthusiastic about "taking the club to the next level." The board temporarily made the benefactor the president of the board and approved the hiring of Sveltlana. Making the benefactor the president was done to expedite the legal paper work of hiring a non-U.S. citizen. This group of board members was very interested in increasing the competitive nature of the club. They wanted more intense workouts and more focus on producing potential national- and Olympic-quality swimmers and were not as concerned about the burn-out factor.

Welliver did his best under the circumstances. It just so happened that his intermediate coach wanted to start a special group for the children who were too fast for the intermediate group, but not mature enough for the senior group. By letting Sveltlana take over the intermediate group, this new group could be formed. It would also allow Sveltlana to get more experience coaching younger children. Also, some good news occurred when the books were finally balanced. The club still owed the school district for pool fees and Welliver for back pay, but the $20,000 error was a simple booking issue and not additional debt.

A substantial number of the parents whose children were coached by Sveltlana seemed to be pleased with the rigor of the workouts. Welliver had to admit that he also had learned some new drills. However, Sveltlana really seemed to have only one coaching style. He felt that with some experience, she could be quite valuable to the entire club once she learned that children of different age groups needed different motivations and coaching styles. He felt she would be ready for that role in a couple of months.

Unfortunately, the board could not wait. The next couple of board meetings were very uncomfortable. Various board members felt that Sveltlana should be used immediately as a floating coach for all the sessions and not be used to staff a particular group — especially one in which their children did not swim. Some parents started switching their kids back from the "super intermediate" group to the intermediate group, just to be with Sveltlana. Board members interrupted Welliver's own coaching sessions to air their complaints. At one point, a board member told Welliver that he should step aside and let Sveltlana become the head coach and threatened that if Welliver didn't agree, then maybe the board should replace him.

This was the last straw, and Welliver decided to resign. Out of solidarity, Tim, the club's intermediate coach, decided to resign as well. Tim was a young college student who had been hired two years earlier. He turned out to be a diamond in the rough in the sense that the school district eventually recognized his skill and hired him to work part time as the swim coach for the other high school in the district. Welliver and Tim turned in their resignations with the agreement that they would stay for two months to end the current swimming cycle. Welliver suggested that his back pay could be paid off by letting his high-school-aged daughter swim in lieu of fees. The benefactor immediately proclaimed that such a small swim club could not afford to pay such a large severance package to a resigning coach.

Before Welliver could speak, Sam, a board member who did live in the school district and who had always been supportive of Welliver, reminded the board that this was back pay officially owed to Welliver, not a "severance package." Sam then resigned from the board that very night, in disgust.

PRESENT EVENTS

The next two months turned out to be even more chaotic. The school district announced that because of a failed school bond initiative, they would be demanding immediate payment of back pool fees and that the rates would go up. The club's board members soon discovered that there had been a lot of economic value in Welliver's leadership. For instance, it was discovered that Welliver's board membership with the state sanctioning body was instrumental in achieving the club's charter and aided its participation in and hosting of sanctioned swim meets. Also, the two resigning coaches were high school coaches within the school district and, thus, had building keys. Now the club would have the additional expense of hiring a district employee to unlock the pool area, stay for the workout and lock the building afterward. Also, if the replacement coaches were not certified lifeguards, as the original coaches were, then lifeguards would have to be hired as well. In the process of juggling all these complications, no recruitment effort took place to get new beginning swimmers into the pipeline, while the senior swimmers started to graduate and leave the club. All in all, the financial outlook for the club began to look very bleak. In reaction to the resignations, a large number of parents, who previously were either apathetic or uninformed about governance issues, started to question the board in person and by petitions. Some parents even withdrew their children from the club.

Eventually, the majority of the board members, including the benefactor, announced that they were going to resign from the board, quit OHNO and start their own swim club with a more intense, Olympic-style goal. They then proceeded to recruit members from OHNO by "cherry picking" almost 20 of the fastest swimmers in the club, and by taking Sveltlana with them. The balance of the donation was now returned to the benefactor. At this point, Welliver and the former intermediate coach agreed to come back, and the club started the process of rebuilding its membership. Though there was a huge drop in enrolled swimmers, the return of the coaching staff and Sveltlana's resignation resulted in savings that gave the club a reasonable financial outlook for the future.

Richard Ivey School of Business
The University of Western Ontario

9B07M007

GVM EXPLORATION LIMITED

Guo-Liang Frank Jiang wrote this case under the supervision of Professor Michael Rouse solely to provide material for class discussion. The authors do not intend to illustrate either effective or ineffective handling of a managerial situation. The authors may have disguised certain names and other identifying information to protect confidentiality.

Version: (A) 2006-12-04

On Monday morning June 27, 2005, Matt Roberts, the engineering manager of GVM Exploration Limited, was preparing for a meeting with the company's CEO and VP Finance. He wondered what action to recommend regarding the weekend blockade by a small group of protesters, consisting mainly of local First Nations people, of the only accessible road to the company's Grizzly Valley coal site in British Columbia, Canada.

CANADA'S MINERAL INDUSTRY AND COAL MINING

Canada's rich natural resources and the industries they supported were a vital part of the country's economy and society. This sector was the lifeblood of hundreds of communities throughout Canada — many of them rural, remote, northern and aboriginal. Forestry, energy, minerals, metals, earth sciences and allied industries accounted for 13 per cent of Canada's GDP and more than 40 per cent of total Canadian exports. Natural resources companies directly employed almost one million Canadians and just as many were employed indirectly.

The mineral industry was a pivotal part of Canada's natural resource economy, representing 3.9 per cent of Canada's total GDP of $1,045 billion[1] in 2004. An improving global economic environment, especially the rapid growth of China and India, had resulted in a period of high commodity prices since 2003. The strong commodity cycle gave a boost to the Canadian mining industry. According to Natural Resources Canada, preliminary estimates for the value of production for all sectors of the Canadian mining industry (excluding crude oil and natural gas) totaled $24.2 billion in 2004, up from $20.1 billion in 2003 and $19.9 billion in 2002. Of this, metal production increased by 29.6 per cent to $12.5 billion and nonmetallic production increased by 12.6 per cent to $10.0 billion. The value of coal increased by 7.1 per cent to $1.6 billion.

---

[1] *All funds in Canadian dollars unless specified otherwise.*

Coal had been mined in Canada on a massive scale. It was Canada's single-most valuable export to Japan. Most coal mining activities took place in Alberta, British Columbia, Saskatchewan and Nova Scotia. The majority of the electricity in Alberta, Saskatchewan and Nova Scotia was generated from coal and the industry created jobs across the country, directly enriching Canada's economy by $5 billion a year.

GVM EXPLORATION LIMITED

Based in Toronto, Ontario, GVM Exploration was a junior mining company listed on the Toronto Stock Exchange with interests in seven mineral deposits and a number of exploration projects in Canada. A junior mining company was a company that undertook exploration and/or mine development activities. Juniors might also have production interests. GVM had five full-time employees and one part-time bookkeeper.

Exploration was the first stage in the coal mining industry. At this stage, new coal deposits and existing coalfields were identified and assessed for quality and quantity of the resource. Though the direct economic impact of exploration activities was quite modest, its long-term potential was high when the future value of new deposits, mining operations and revenues were considered. The second stage was development. Social, economic, logistical and environmental plans were prepared and reviewed by various stakeholders at this stage. These plans were designed with input from local residents, environmental agencies, government departments, corporate managers and consultants. This input helped ensure that the construction and operation of mines were sensitive to stakeholders' needs. Successful exploration and development led to the production stage, which included coal mining and processing. Almost all of the jobs, much of the investment, and most of the operating costs occurred at this stage. Production was the economic heart of the coal industry.

A junior mining company operated primarily on the basis of funding its activities by selling shares on a stock market. Juniors lacked the self-sustaining cash flow of major mining companies. Investors who bought shares of a junior hoped that the company would find a deposit or make a deal with a major company, which might increase the share price. A junior company also offered an opportunity for investors to profit if the company transformed itself into a mid-tier or senior mining company. A senior mining company generally had much larger market capitalization and had the capability to take over viable projects and to develop major mines.

GVM Exploration's principal assets were the "world class" Grizzly Valley anthracite coal deposits in southeast British Columbia, and the Dovik Creek gold-cobalt-bismuth deposit in northern Quebec. These two major projects were undergoing various technical, environmental and feasibility assessments by hired contractors and consultants. Commercial production had not begun at either the Grizzly Valley or Dovik Creek projects and GVM was making the transition from an exploration company to a producer. Grizzly Valley was scheduled to begin production in 2008 and Dovik Creek in 2009. GVM completed a $20 million equity financing in December 2004 (see Exhibit 1). Its market value was approximately $119 million at the end of June 2005, with 34 million shares outstanding and no debt.

GRIZZLY VALLEY PROJECT

GVM owned a 100 per cent interest in the Grizzly Valley anthracite coal project in southeast British Columbia. The Grizzly Valley lease was purchased in 2002 from a Canadian subsidiary of a large oil company which conducted exploration and test mining programs, spending approximately $65 million developing the project. The Grizzly Valley project straddled a rail right-of-way and roadbed which provided road access to a provincial highway. However, due to extreme weather conditions, the Grizzly Valley site was only practically accessible between May and early November. A new road was proposed by GVM to connect the mine site to the closest town along the highway. The potential mine site was located within the territory of a First Nations group[2].

The Grizzly Valley site included four major deposits which collectively contained coal resources of 108 million tonnes classified as Measured, 123 million tonnes classified as Indicated, 2.57 billion tonnes in the Inferred and Speculative classes. Grizzly Valley contained one of the world's largest undeveloped resources of high rank anthracite coal.

Anthracite is a "hard coal" with the highest rank, carbon and energy content, and lowest moisture and volatile content of all coals. Only about one per cent of world coal reserves were anthracite grade. Unique properties made anthracite suitable for use in a broad range of metallurgical, thermal, water purification and composite materials applications. The most important new market for Grizzly Valley anthracite was pulverized coal injection (PCI) coal used in the steel industry. Anthracite was also a preferred fuel source for new "clean coal" technologies for power generation that reduced greenhouse gas emissions. In addition, the high cost of oil was making coal-to-oil liquification technologies economically attractive. World annual production of anthracite was in excess of 350 million tonnes. Prices ranged between US$50 and US$250/tonne with metallurgical products selling for between US$70 and US$130/tonne, and filter media at US$250/tonne.

DOVIK CREEK PROJECT

GVM Exploration's 90 per cent-owned Dovik Creek project in northern Quebec was a significant deposit of cobalt, containing approximately one million ounces of by-product gold and it was one of the largest known resources of bismuth in the world. Cobalt was a high-strength, magnetic metal and it was in increasing demand for a variety of chemical and metallurgical applications. The largest growth in the cobalt market was in the chemicals industry for the manufacture of rechargeable batteries, catalysts, audio recording tape, pigments and food additives. The global cobalt market was about 49,500 tonnes per year. Annual growth in the cobalt market had averaged between five and six per cent for the past two decades. Prices had generally been in the range of US$15 to US$25/pound for the past two years.

Bismuth was a relatively uncommon metal with unique properties, including very high density and low melting temperature. Bismuth was also quite inert and scientifically recognized as one of the safest metals, making it ideally suited for numerous pharmaceuticals, medicines, cosmetics and medical devices. Significant growth in the bismuth market was accelerating because it had physical properties similar to lead but was non-toxic. Bismuth was replacing lead in a number of applications due to increasing concern for the environment. Current worldwide consumption of bismuth was approximately 7,000 tonnes per year and had been growing at approximately 10 per cent per year. The market was constrained by supply and, ironically, most bismuth was sourced as a by-product from lead mining, which suggested that further decreases in lead consumption would also have an impact on bismuth supply. The long-term price of bismuth had averaged approximately US$4/pound. According to a 2005 research report the in-ground value of the metal content of Dovik Creek resources totaled $2.0 billion.

GVM had recently entered into an agreement to purchase a used mill from another Canadian mining company. The mill was well-suited for use at Dovik Creek and would significantly reduce projected

---

[2] *The name of the First Nation is not provided to maintain the company's confidentiality.*

capital costs for the development. GVM would purchase the buildings, major equipment and approximately $2 million in inventory for $3.3 million. A revised feasibility study reflecting the acquisition of this equipment was expected to be completed in mid-2006. Upon the expected closing of the deal in 2006, GVM would have three years to remove the assets to Dovik Creek. Meanwhile, GVM was working on a second transaction to acquire additional equipment. GVM was also planning to conduct a $9.5 million underground bulk sampling program at Dovik Creek in 2006.

FIRST NATIONS

First Nations refers to any of the numerous aboriginal groups formally recognized by the Canadian government under the federal Indian Act of 1876. First Nation was a legally undefined term that came into common usage in the 1970s to replace the term "Indian band." A band was defined as a body of aboriginals for whose collective use and benefit lands had been set apart or money had been held by the Canadian Crown; alternatively, such a group was declared to be a band for the purposes of the Indian Act. There are over 600 First Nations governments or bands in Canada. Roughly half of these are located in the provinces of Ontario and British Columbia.

In general, the Canadian government provided a strong legislative and political framework for indigenous rights protection. The government's aboriginal policy evolved over the years from an effort to acculturate and assimilate indigenous peoples to one supporting indigenous self-determination and cultural expression. Since 1763, First Nations had ceded their lands to the Crown in return for other benefits. However, British Columbia had adopted different land rights policies. Most of the lands the B.C. First Nations inhabited had never been ceded. No treaties had been signed. Claims to land title were ambiguous in many First Nations areas.

Canada had a strong record of protecting the environment and the interests of native people while developing the natural resources sector to achieve economic and social benefits. Increasingly, mining companies were taking into account their impact on society through the products they made, the people they employed and the communities in which they worked. However, First Nations issues remained a salient challenge in the mining industry. There were many land access issues. On one hand, the industry and government were making efforts to involve aboriginal peoples. On the other hand, the companies, especially junior firms, continued to feel pressures dealing with native issues. Lack of guidance was attributed to the continuous disputes. The following comment was made by a mining executive at a meeting organized by the Finance and Economic Affairs Committee of the Legislative Assembly of Ontario:

> There doesn't seem to be a set process to work with the First Nations communities and to make a determination of whether or not there are land issues, so it would definitely be beneficial to get some clarification and guidance on how we can walk through the process. We definitely want to do that. We are very interested in making sure all the stakeholders are taken care of, but without guidance it's difficult to determine what is adequate for our permitting and consultation.

GRIZZLY VALLEY FIRST NATIONS

The Grizzly Valley area First Nation refers to a group of aboriginal people whose traditional territories are in southeast British Columbia. Historically, they were a nomadic people, traveling around their area with the seasons and their food supply. Each spring and summer, they traditionally returned to the Grizzly

Valley area to fish. Today, they are a small nation of approximately 6,000 persons with all but 800 of their members living outside the traditional territory.

They are comprised of two bands, each with an elected council which comes under the jurisdiction of the local Central Council (CC). The CC was comprised of representatives of 10 families from each band. The CC linked the Grizzly Valley bands and had represented them on issues of joint concern, specifically on asserting inherent rights and title. The CC was a registered society under the B.C. Society Act. The government of British Columbia had been engaged in negotiations with the CC and local bands on a consultation and accommodation agreement on forestry, mining, oil and gas.

However, the CC faced challenges from a small group within the nation. Grizzly Valley Hereditary Chiefs (Elders) had been holding a protest against their leadership for several months and had occupied the office of the elected chief. The Elders also questioned the pace of development. They claimed that the proposed development of a number of resource projects was too fast. The CC was perceived by the Elders to be overly pro-business. The Elders insisted that they participate in the decision-making process.

On January 13, 2005, in response to news that a 160-km industrial road would be built in the area, 35 Elders occupied the band office and asserted their right to speak for their people. They were responding to information that the CC had signed a deal with the province to facilitate mining, logging and hydroelectricity projects in exchange for $250,000 per year for the Council. For many, it was the first time they had received official information about so many industrial projects. Their principal concern was that their land, resources and rights were being sold without their knowledge. The Elders agreed to stand strong to protect the land for future generations. They demanded the resignation of the elected CC leader. He was accused of abusing his elected position in order to promote his own businesses. They demanded that the CC reconsider the agreement with the B.C. government, which they feared would fast-track numerous major projects in the region. These projects included two copper-gold mine projects, a coal bed methane project, and GVM Exploration's Grizzly Valley coal mine project.

On Saturday February 12, the Elders announced a moratorium that prohibited any resource development on local lands until more representative and accountable leadership and governance was achieved. At a meeting on March 10, the Elders delivered the moratorium to representatives of a major oil company. The next day, in support of the moratorium, one of the First Nations bands, along with its Hereditary Chiefs Council and band council, dressed in traditional regalia and formally requested the oil company to leave their territory. The company subsequently cancelled their 2005 field exploration program.

ROAD BLOCKADE

On Saturday June 25, a group of Elders, and First Nations' families blockaded the entrance to the road which connected the Grizzly Valley site and the rail roadbed and eventually led to the main highway (Exhibit 2). The blockade prevented GVM and other exploration companies from sending in heavy industrial equipment. It also disrupted the business of local tour companies.

The protesters claimed that GVM's project infringed upon Aboriginal Title and Rights when the company was granted tenure without honorable consultation with the family on whose traditional territory the tenure was located. They felt that, because of the breakdown in band leadership, it would be appropriate for GVM to engage directly with the people who would be most affected by the proposed development. A leader of the protest noted,

The GVM Exploration project in the area would directly impact our traditional lifestyle, a lifestyle we've maintained for tens of thousands of years and to date we continue to use this area on a regular basis. Matter of fact a few of our campsites are set to be flooded with waste dumps. However, no one will destroy our world without first consulting with us.

Although the Elders had demanded the resignation of the elected leader since January 2005, some protestors and supporters asserted that the blockade had nothing to do with their resignation demands. They stated that the issue was not just about mining or resource extraction either. Rather, the issue was the protection of the traditional territory, heritage sites and lifestyle from the destruction of non-renewable resource extraction. It was about sustainable development. It was about the inherent rights of traditional peoples to govern their territories as they had for millennia.

MATT ROBERTS

Matt Roberts started to work at GVM Exploration after he earned an MBA degree from a leading Canadian business school. He had significant experience in energy, metals and industrial minerals projects, having held positions in mine operations and engineering with multiple firms.

Roberts was deeply concerned about the blockade because GVM was unable to mobilize its camp to support a $2 million environmental assessment project. Roberts was worried about the lack of time available to complete the work if the blockade was not lifted. Due to extreme weather conditions, the Grizzly Valley site was really only accessible between May and early November. It would take five months to complete the 2005 work program, gathering baseline data to support the project's application to the B.C. environmental agency. If GVM could not enter the site to perform environmental tests that summer, they would have to wait until May 2006. Their commercial production would be delayed for at least nine months and possibly an entire year (see Exhibit 3). Unlike major mining companies which often had separate departments dedicated to native issues, a junior company like GVM usually could not afford the time and lacked the depth of experience of the majors. The process could last several years. Roberts wondered what the financial implications of the blockade would be, both on the work program and on the company's share price. The valuation of GVM largely hinged on the Grizzly Valley coal project. Thanks to the strong demand from Asian markets, metallurgical coal was selling for record prices in 2005 (see Exhibit 4). Any delay of the project was going to send a negative signal to its shareholders and the investment community.

Roberts wondered if the company should fight for an injunction in court. However, he felt uncomfortable about the idea. The police might make arrests if the protestors did not cooperate and the possibility of violence and the threat to public safety was a concern. In addition, GVM had been quite cautious in the negotiations with the Central Council and promised to develop a constructive relationship with local communities. Roberts was concerned that a confrontation might undermine these prior efforts. Further complicating the issue was the growing internal dispute amongst the First Nations peoples, leaving GVM in a difficult position.

Roberts doubted that the B.C. government would directly intervene in this incident. He felt that the B.C. government had generally stepped away from native issues and left them up to the companies to work out, although it was trying to create a business-friendly environment for the mining industry. Many thought the previous government's policies had discouraged resource development in the province. Roberts knew that lack of communication might be a contributing factor to the current situation. He was wondering if additional communication and negotiation would help solve the problem.

Roberts did think, however, that GVM was not in a completely passive position. The CC had always been supportive of the coal mine project. GVM planned to enter into an Impact and Benefits Agreements with the Grizzly Valley and other First Nations where operations might impact their traditional territories. The protesters were supported by a relatively small group of people within the Grizzly Valley First Nation. Many others did not support the blockade. Actually, local First Nations' companies had been directly engaged in environmental studies at Grizzly Valley. GVM retained two local First Nations environmental service companies to collect environmental data and to assist the company with permitting of the project. If the blockade continued, 60 jobs could be lost, along with a $1.5-million contract. Down the road, commercial production would generate a significantly larger number of employment opportunities in the region.

All along, GVM's strategy was to develop the Dovik Creek project independently into production stage and to secure partners to develop the Grizzly Valley project. Production at Dovik Creek would immediately increase GVM's workforce by 300. More importantly, GVM would need approximately $200 million to finance the transformation of the Dovik Creek project. The Grizzly Valley project was on an even larger scale. It had been estimated that GVM would spend $275 million to put the largest Grizzly Valley deposit into production to produce an initial 1.5 million tonnes of ultra-low volatile PCI coal. In the second year of production, a further $158 million would be spent to expand the production to 3.0 million tonnes per year. Some companies had expressed interest in the Grizzly Valley project but there had been no serious negotiations.

Roberts knew he would have to consider GVM's options carefully and present a reasonable plan at the afternoon's meeting.

Exhibit 1

CONSOLIDATE BALANCE SHEETS

As at December 31	2004	2003
ASSETS		
Current assets		
Cash and cash equivalents	$ 24,642,774	$ 3,348,384
Short-term investments	268,872	1,269,154
Accounts receivable	446,629	132,173
Prepaid expenses	17,865	13,275
	25,376,140	4,762,986
Reclamation bond	225,900	210,000
Investment in and advances to affiliated company	379,440	370,661
Capital assets, net	19,355	9,420
Interests in mining properties	3,153,280	3,153,280
Deferred exploration expenditures	11,296,536	9,156,715
	40,450,651	**17,663,062**
LIABILITIES AND SHAREHOLDERS' EQUITY		
Current liabilities		
Accounts payable and accrued liabilities	676,405	113,919
Income taxes payable	83,235	60,938
Total current liabilities	**759,640**	**174,857**
Future income taxes	4,000,000	2,660,000
Total liabilities	**4,749,640**	**2,834,857**
SHAREHOLDERS' EQUITY		
Share capital	36,179,828	14,804,848
Contributed surplus	1,348,840	522,146
Deficit	(1,837,657)	(498,789)
	35,691,011	**14,828,205**
	40,450,651	**17,663,062**

Source: GVM Exploration Limited, 2005 Annual Report.

Exhibit 2

THE ROAD BLOCKADE

Source: GVM Exploration Limited, Corporate Archive.

Exhibit 3

GRIZZLY VALLEY PROJECT ACTIVITY SCHEDULE

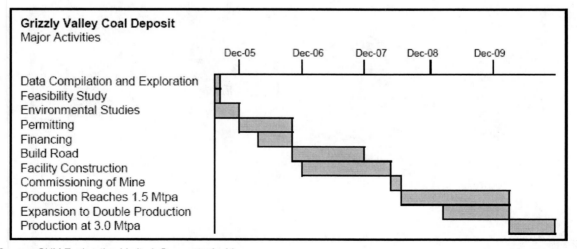

Source: GVM Exploration Limited, Corporate Archive.

Exhibit 4

AVERAGE METALLURGICAL COAL PRICE

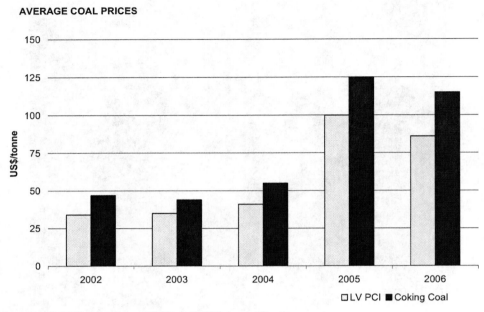

AVERAGE COAL PRICES

□ LV PCI ■ Coking Coal

Note: LV PCI = Low-volatile PCI coal. Data of 2005 and 2006 were estimation.
Source: GVM Minerals Limited, 2005 Annual Report.

THOMSON GREENHOUSE

D. Wesley Balderson
University of Lethbridge

Background

Thomson Greenhouse is located just outside Sudbury, Ontario, and is owned by Earl and Lisa Thomson. It is a seasonal operation, offering many different types of bedding plants, vegetables, annuals, perennials, and specialty plants and arrangements. The business also has a two-acre tree nursery and garden offering a wide range of trees from pines to fruit trees.

Earl and Lisa Thomson have been operating the business for 17 years after taking over the business from Lisa's parents. The original business was located on land on the outskirts of Sudbury that was annexed by the city. It was at that time that Earl and Lisa decided to move from the city to a small acreage, so that they could continue the business and set up a new location. The structures were taken down and reassembled on the new acreage just northeast of Sudbury.

Much of the knowledge of the greenhouse business has been passed down from Lisa's parents and as Earl and Lisa have three sons working in the business it continues to be a solely family-run operation. Many of the aspects of the business have remained the same since it was established. Thomson Greenhouse has been serving the city of Sudbury and surrounding area for many years and has been fairly successful in establishing a name for quality products and good customer service.

Thomson Greenhouse is a form of second income to the Thomsons due to its seasonal nature and because Earl is the chief accountant for a local manufacturing company. It also has allowed the Thomsons' three sons to work in the business to help finance their schooling. The oldest son, Derek, is currently about to graduate with a bachelor's degree in business from the local university while the other brothers (Ryan and Russel) are in Grades 10 and 12 respectively. Lisa's parents, Morris and Anna Slemko, also work in the business during the busy times.

Due to the success of the business and the fact that their sons are getting to the age where they are about to leave home the Thomsons are faced with some long-term decisions about the business.

Organization

Thomson Greenhouse is a general partnership with the two partners being Earl and Lisa Thomson. Earl feels that although they have unlimited liability under this arrangement, the tax and flexibility advantages of a partnership outweigh this risk. Both partners own an equal share of the business, although Lisa spends more time working in the business because Earl has a full-time job in Sudbury.

Earl and Lisa have equal authority with regard to the employees. Both are knowledgeable regarding horticulture and care for trees and plants. Earl is more responsible for the accounting, advertising, deliveries, and seeding. Lisa handles orders, daily operations in the greenhouse, transplanting, sales, and customer service. Both Earl and Lisa know their strengths and weaknesses, and tend to do the things they each do well. Some overlapping occurs, but this is advantageous in some ways because some operations are too big to handle by themselves.

Over the years there have been few conflicts in the management of the operation or with employees as it has all been within the family. All three of the Thomson sons have worked in the business throughout the summer as well as evenings and weekends for a number of years. During the busy season Lisa's parents, from whom Earl and Lisa purchased the business, help out. Because of the fact that the business is family owned and operated, no formal personnel policies or training programs have been developed. Management of the company has been carried out on an informal basis. The employees are paid on a straight salary basis with considerable flexibility available for the sons as things come up that they need to do.

One of the major concerns that Earl and Lisa have is the future of the business when the children finish their high school and university studies. The business is not currently large enough to be a full-time occupation unless a considerable capital investment is made to expand the operation. Another difficulty is that the second-oldest son, Ryan, has expressed interest in becoming involved in the business but the Thomsons are concerned about how to make this transition should it take place. They are wondering what effects such a move would have on their other two sons.

Location and Physical Facilities

Thomson Greenhouse is located just northeast of the city limits of Sudbury. The market area not only includes the city of Sudbury (population 90,000) but also many of the small communities around the city, which is estimated to have another 60,000 people. This location serves Thomson well because of its proximity to the city; as well, its rural location allows for plenty of space for production and expansion, if required. Distribution is carried out primarily by truck, and the highways and roads in the area are very well maintained.

Thomson Greenhouse is located on 20 acres of which 5 are used for the greenhouse and the Thomsons' residence and the other 15 are rented out to a local farmer. The greenhouse building covers approximately 800 square metres. Although most of the area is taken up with plants and could be referred to as selling space, a small area at the front is devoted to customer service and a cash counter. A small greenhouse at the back is used for personal items and the holding of special orders. The building's age is a concern, and it has begun deteriorating. The frame is made of wood and the aging process has damaged many of the wooden glass frames. Much of the material for this greenhouse came from the original greenhouse that was moved from the previous site.

Recently Thomson Greenhouse purchased a new computer system. The Thomsons are in the process of converting their manual record keeping and inventory control over to the computer. Other equipment owned by the business are a small front-end loader/garden tractor, a truck used to deliver plants to commercial customers, roto tiller, dirt mixer, and dirt purifier, and other miscellaneous garden tools and greenhouses devices.

Purchasing for Thomson Greenhouse is carried out by both Earl and Lisa. They purchase their supply of inventory from various seed processors located primarily in Southern Ontario and the United States. Quality, dependability, and price are all used to evaluate suppliers. Lead times for ordering are about 30 days for most items. No formal inventory-ordering method is used as the business is small enough that Earl and Lisa are able to adjust their inventory levels from visual inspection and from previous experience.

Marketing

The target market for Thomson Greenhouse consists of consumers who come to the greenhouse as well as some large retail accounts to supermarkets such as Superstore and A&P. The consumer market tends to be older, those who have the resources and time to spend on their yards and gardens. The supermarket or commercial accounts purchase vegetables and some flowers while those customers who come out to Thomson Greenhouse make greater purchases of bedding plants and trees. In terms of quality and price, the commercial accounts tend to be interested in low price. As a result, the margins that Thomson achieves with the commercial accounts are much lower than with the customer accounts. Those who come out to the greenhouse desire high quality and customer service even if it means paying a slightly higher price. Earl Thomson realizes this and sets prices to meet these preferences and also to ensure that the business is able to achieve a profit. The profit margin has to be high enough to include the discounts that inevitably occur at the end of the season due to the perishability of the product.

The busy time of year for bedding plants is during May and June as most people are preparing their yards and gardens. During the summer and fall, produce sales increase, and during the winter months very little business is done.

There are several other greenhouses in the Sudbury area and many customers do price shopping. Thomson Greenhouse has always prided itself on superior customer service and despite the competitive nature of the industry seems to retain a fairly loyal following. The commercial contracts also add to the stability of operations for Thomson. Earl has an informal idea of Thomson Greenhouse market share through the monitoring of sales of their various products.

One of the trends the Thomsons have noticed is the increasing market share that has been obtained in the gardening-nursery product category by department stores such as Wal-Mart and Canadian Tire. Thomson Greenhouse currently has contracts with only two supermarkets and although these have provided steady volumes, purchases from these sources have not grown over the past few years. The Thomsons are considering attempting to obtain contracts with some of these department stores as a means of increasing sales. They realize that margins would be thin, however, and that price would be a major purchasing factor for the consumer. Many of the other greenhouses in the area are actively competing for the business of these stores and the Thomsons realize that they would have to be very competitive to be successful in obtaining a contract. If they were able to secure new purchasers, expansion of their current operation would seem to be necessary.

Thomson Greenhouse uses several forms of promotion. It places some ads in the local newspaper and utilizes the Yellow Pages. It also purchases a booth at the Home and Garden Tradeshow, which is held in Sudbury each spring. Occasionally, direct mail promotion is used to highlight special sales or end-of-season discounts. Thomson uses business cards and has been actively involved in sponsoring minor hockey teams and karate schools as part of its public relations promotion. Earl and Lisa realize, however, that word of mouth is their most effective form of promotion so they ensure that they and their sales staff are knowledgeable about the product and courteous to the customer.

Financial Situation

Thomson Greenhouse has been profitable since its establishment, earning about $10,000 per year on about $40,000 in sales. (See Exhibit 1 for the latest income statement.) Although sales haven't increased over the past five years, Earl and Lisa have not been concerned about this because there has been an increase in competition and they are currently operating at capacity with their present facilities. They have been using a one-book system for accounting but are currently switching over to an accounting software program in conjunction with their computer purchase.

One of the concerns that Earl and Lisa have is the state of their current greenhouse, which is getting old. They are considering constructing a new one in addition to the current greenhouse. This would increase the capacity of the business and would allow for increased sales but would also increase the workload for the Thomsons, something that they are not sure they want. Alternatively, they could replace the existing greenhouse and maintain current operations but at a more efficient level.

A new greenhouse of a similar size to the current one would cost approximately $12,000 and would last about 10 years. If the Thomsons decided to go ahead with this, they would finance $8,000 at the local bank at 8 percent interest. They estimate that the annual sales for a greenhouse of this size would be $30,000.

Exhibit 1

Thomson Greenhouse
Income Statement
For the Year Ended December 31, 2004

Revenue		$37,000
Expenses		
Cost of Goods Sold		
Seed and materials	$3,560	
Containers	3,150	
Fertilizer	290	
Water	305	
Soil	90	
Direct labour	3,000	$10,395
Contribution Margin		26,605
Occupancy and Selling Costs		
Building repairs	130	
Truck costs	2,300	
Office expenses	1,015	
Property taxes	1,560	
Heat and power	3,450	
Advertising	2,150	
Selling labour	3,150	
Depreciation	$3,800	$17,555
Profit before Income Taxes		$9,050

Thomsom Greenhouse
Balance Sheet
As at December 31, 2004

Current Assets		
Cash	$ 1,000	
Accounts receivable	1,500	
Inventory	3,000	
Fixed Assets		
Land	26,000	
Buildings	58,000	
Equipment	$ 21,000	
Total Assets		$110,500
Liabilities and Owner's Equity		
Liabilities		
Accounts Payable	1,500	
Owner's Equity	$109,000	
Total Liabilities and Owner's Equity		$110,500

Questions

1. Discuss the implications of the Thomsons' attempt to obtain additional commercial contracts (the department stores) for their products.
2. Evaluate the decision to construct another greenhouse from a financial as well as organizational point of view. (Use rate of return, payback, and break-even analysis in your evaluation.)
3. Comment on the financial health of the Thomson Greenhouse through a review of the financial statements.
4. Discuss the implications for succession of the business if the decision were to
   a. pass the business to one of the sons
   b. sell the business to someone outside the family

CLOVIS JEWELLERS

D. Wesley Balderson
University of Lethbridge

Clovis Jewellers is a small jewellery store located in Brandon, Manitoba.[1] You have been called on by the owner to prepare an analysis of the business. The owners have supplied you with a detailed description of their operation and strategy. Critically evaluate each area described in the case.

Structure

Legal Structure. Clovis Jewellers is an incorporated company under the name of Clovis Jewellers (1978) Limited. It is a privately held corporation. The only shareholders are Mr. and Mrs. Neudorf, each of whom owns 50 percent of the outstanding shares. As a corporation, Clovis Jewellers is authorized to issue an unlimited number of Class A, B, and C common shares. The only outstanding shares are 100 Class A shares. In the case of Clovis Jewellers, the shareholders are the owners, directors, and managers.

Financial Structure. The capital structure of Clovis Jewellers is financed by a combination of debt and shareholder's equity. The debt constitutes roughly 75 percent of the capital and the shareholder's equity the other 25 percent. The shareholder's equity is made up of both class A share capital and retained earnings, of which the latter is by far the larger.

The debt financing is held with the Bank of Montreal and is in the form of a long-term loan. This loan is approximately $190,000. The first $150,000 is guaranteed through a provincial government small business assistance plan and therefore carries an interest rate of 9 percent; the remaining $40,000 carries a rate of prime plus 1 percent. This long-term debt is covered by personal guarantees of Fred Meyer, a business associate of Mr. Neudorf, and by a mortgage on the Neudorfs' house.

The bank of Montreal has also authorized an operating line of credit to Clovis Jewellers with a ceiling of $20,000. This line of credit is used to assist Mr. Neudorf in managing the cash flow in the slower summer months.

Organizational Structure. There are four levels of employees in Clovis Jewellers' organizational structure (see Appendix 1 on page 464). The first level is the manager and is filled by Mr. Neudorf. The duties of this position include accounting and financial management, management of day-to-day store operations and gemologist/diamond expert. Mr. Neudorf works together with both the assistant manager and the sales staff.

The second level in the organization is the assistant manager and is filled by Mrs. Neudorf. She works as the assistant manager approximately 50 percent of the time and as a salesperson the remaining 50 percent. The duties of the assistant manager include purchasing of merchandise and control of inventory. The inventory control function is done on a very informal basis, usually by a simple visual check.

The third level in the organization includes the sales staff and the repair service administrator. The job of overseeing the repair service is held by one of the full-time salespersons and requires approximately 20 percent of her time. The number of salespersons varies with the time of year, ranging from six to seven at Christmastime to two or three during the summer months.

The fourth level in the organization is the goldsmith and repairperson. This position is filled by Mr. Neudorf and requires a great deal of his time. Mr. Neudorf works together with the repair service administrator when acting as goldsmith.

---

1 Although this case describes an actual business, the names of the business and owners, as well as the location, have been changed.

There are two positions outside of the four-level organization. One is an accountant, and the other is a lawyer. Mr. Neudorf hires these two professionals on a part-time basis as demand calls for them. Both the accountant and the lawyer interact only with Mr. Neudorf.

Personnel

Clovis Jewellers experiences very little employee turnover (one staff member every two or three years) and therefore does not engage in recruiting procedures on a regular basis. When a new staff member is needed, a small advertisement is placed in the classified section of Brandon's daily newspaper. Although an advertisement is always placed, most hiring results through word of mouth and other contacts with neighbouring businesspeople.

When selecting a new employee, Mr. and Mrs. Neudorf look for individuals with an outgoing, friendly personality. Usually the person is middle-aged and has sales experience. Application forms are screened based on these qualifications, and the applicant who best meets the qualifications is asked to come in for a personal interview. Unless there is more than one "ideal" applicant, the new employee is hired after only one interview.

The training supplied to new employees comes in two forms: product training and operations training. The product training requires the employee to learn a great deal about jewellery—a very complex area. The individual must gain knowledge about watches, diamonds, gemstones, and qualities of gold. This product training occurs as the person works in the showroom selling jewellery and takes approximately one month.

The operations training is less involved than the product training and is completed in the first week or two of employment. This training involves learning the daily routine carried out at Clovis Jewellers, as well as cash register and receipt-writing operations.

The method of employee remuneration is a straight hourly wage; no commissions are paid. Employees' hours are recorded in a payroll register, and employees are paid every two weeks based on the number of hours worked. Mr. Neudorf tried to introduce a commission pay plan in the past, but employee resistance forced him to shelve the plan.

Employee morale appears relatively high compared with other retail stores. Mr. Neudorf believes this is because he and his wife treat the sales staff with respect and as friends. The employees know the importance of selling to the company's well-being, and Mr. Neudorf continually reinforces this by verbally acknowledging an individual for his or her sales efforts. A further indication of high morale is the fact that Clovis Jewellers experiences an extremely low rate of absenteeism and lateness.

Marketing

Product. A majority of Clovis Jewellers' yearly sales consists of ring and precious stone jewellery; for this reason, its product mix heavily favours these two items. Ring sales are responsible for the single highest sales total; therefore, great emphasis is placed on the ring inventory when the product mix is evaluated. Clovis Jewellers is known for carrying good-quality merchandise; this is reflected in the purchasing habits and quality control employed at Clovis. However, Clovis has shifted to a lower-quality selection of rings and jewellery to compete with the competition. This shift appears to be temporary, as the better-quality lines remain.

Mr. Neudorf believes seasonal fluctuations in sales do not seriously affect the product mix. Relative sales of most items remain constant throughout the year.

Distribution. Clovis Jewellers is in the middle of a transition from using a traditional manufacturer-retailer distribution channel to a more direct channel. Jewellery and ring manufacturers are actually intermediaries in the supply of diamonds and precious gems (the manufacturers buy the gemstones from large diamond and gemstone suppliers). This method of purchasing was more convenient for Mr. Neudorf but inevitably meant higher-priced merchandise. Mr. Neudorf has now made arrangements to buy diamonds directly from the source of supply and therefore has greatly reduced merchandise costs. This shift also gives Mr. Neudorf much greater control over diamond and gemstone quality.

Pricing. Mr. Neudorf uses several different methods in calculating the retail prices of the merchandise. Brand-name items such as watches are priced according to the manufacturer's suggested retail price, because Mr. Neudorf thinks customers will base their purchase decisions solely on price when shopping for brand names.

Merchandise whose quality the customer cannot differentiate easily, such as gold chains, are priced very competitively. Comparisons are often made with other jewellery stores to ensure that these items are priced competitively. Jewellery items such as earrings and pendants are priced according to a standard markup of keystone (50 percent), plus an additional 10 percent to make up for markdowns, which are often needed to sell the jewellery.

Mr. Neudorf finds rings the hardest items to price, as they carry no brand names or identifying trademarks. Each ring is priced individually, based on special features (or lack of them). A general markup formula is still used, but individual factors dictate the final selling price of the ring. For example, everyday solitaire engagement rings are priced below the standard markup, whereas individual modern engagement rings are priced above that markup.

Promotion. Clovis Jewellers uses a wide range of media in its advertising program, including a daily newspaper, a local television station, AM and FM radio stations, and flyers. Advertising is used to convey both a specific promotional method and corporate image advertising. Mr. Neudorf prepares much of his own advertising, especially radio and newspaper ads. He also gives the ads a personal touch by recording many of the radio ads himself and including his picture in several newspaper advertisements. Mr. Neudorf claims that Clovis Jewellers targets its selling toward middle-aged women, but this target is not evident in the advertising; rather, the advertising appears to be general, with no real objectives or target market in mind. The advertising budget is prepared by taking a percentage of projected sales. This target percentage is between 4 percent and 5 percent.

Mr. Neudorf uses many different forms of sales promotion throughout the year. These include diamond remount plans, jewellery repair sales, graduation promotions, Mother's Day promotions, and other general markdown sales. The number of sales promotions has increased over the past few years due to an increase in competition. The trend in promotions has switched from using them to enhance slow selling periods toward bettering higher selling periods. That is, they are now timed in conjunction with a month of already higher-than-average sales.

Personal selling is heavily used at Clovis Jewellers. Mr. Neudorf believes jewellery requires a substantial selling push and therefore uses in-store personal selling as a major marketing tool. Emphasis is on making every sale count, large or small. Monthly sales totals are updated every day and then compared with the projected sales for the month. This information is then passed on to the salespeople to keep them aware of the importance of selling.

Public relations can also be an effective marketing tool, especially in a close-knit community such as Brandon. Mr. Neudorf is involved with many community clubs and events, which give him a fair amount of low-cost public relations. Clovis Jewellers sponsors sporting events for persons with disabilities and is a member of both the Rotary Club of Brandon and the Brandon Chamber of Commerce (of which Mr. Neudorf has been president and is currently a director). Mr. Neudorf gives talks to local women's groups and at high school career days. He has also had much interaction with the Brandon City Council and has served on committees such as the Brandon Parking Commission.

Location and Layout

Location. Clovis Jewellers' trading area consists of the city of Brandon, surrounding towns and farmlands, and small communities that extend to the Ontario and Saskatchewan borders. The population of the area is slightly greater than 200,000, of which 55,000 live in the city of Brandon. The primary trading area (approximately 70 percent of the business) includes the entire city of Brandon and the surrounding towns of Virden, Souris, Minnedosa, and Neepawa.

The economy of Clovis Jewellers' trading area relies heavily on its two industries, farming and oil. Clovis Jewellers' sales experience large fluctuations due to the characteristics of each of these industries. The downturn in the oil industry has had a significant impact on the firm's profitability; sales have dropped significantly in the past three years.

Clovis Jewellers leases its site from a management firm located in Winnipeg. The basic rent is approximately $2,400 per month. On top of this expense, Clovis pays a yearly management, property tax, and insurance fee for the building. The building is a single-storey structure located on Brandon's main downtown artery. The physical characteristics of the site follow the image Clovis is trying to portray; the storefront is pleasant and modern looking.

The buildings surrounding Clovis Jewellers host mostly banks and other independent retail stores. Several retail stores on the same city block appeal to Clovis's target market, including the Roset by Reid jewellery store located across the street. There is one vacant space on the street, located right next to Clovis Jewellers. The vacancy was caused by a fire over a year ago, and the building remains boarded up.

Clovis Jewellers is located on Ross Street, which is the centre downtown street. Ross Street has angle parking on both sides and is busy every weekday from 9:00 a.m. until around 6:00 p.m. This heavy vehicle traffic is due to the large number of banks in the area that deal with a high volume of customers every day. Ross Street also experiences a high volume of pedestrian traffic during the day, as it is situated in the heart of Brandon's retail and office sector.

Layout. Clovis Jewellers' present location is 1,000 square feet. Eight hundred square feet are used as selling space and the remaining 200 for office and storage space. The showroom is divided among rings, gold chains, watches, gift items, diamond jewellery, and regular jewellery. Although space is allocated to each section according to proportion of total sales, the allocation is based on rough estimates of both percentage of sales and space used.

The layout of the store is designed to make efficient use of high-traffic areas. The engagement rings, which are classified as specialty goods, are located at the back of the store, a spot that would normally see low-traffic volume. The shopping goods such as watches and gold chains are located in high-traffic areas around the cash register and front entrance.

Merchandise is displayed in either a locked showcase or behind a showcase out of the customer's reach. This method of displaying is necessary due to the high value and small size of individual pieces of merchandise. Each display case is lighted by two spotlights dropped from the ceiling. Florescent lights light the general-purpose areas of the store; other lamps are suspended from the ceiling as part of the decor. The lighting appears adequate, as the store gives a "bright" first impression.

Purchasing and Inventory Control

Purchasing. Mrs. Neudorf is responsible for purchasing the majority of the required merchandise. The salespeople often assist her, especially when the purchasing is done in Clovis Jewellers' showroom. Purchasing is done through a combination of jewellery and gift show attendance and meetings with individual supplier representatives.

The tradeshows Mr. and Mrs. Neudorf attend are held throughout Canada and the United States and include cities such as Hawaii, Vancouver, Brandon, Calgary, Winnipeg, and Toronto. Roughly 20 percent of total purchases are made at these tradeshows. Mr. and Mrs. Neudorf attend them for the purpose of obtaining new products and ideas as well as the actual purchasing.

Eighty percent of purchasing is done in-store and with the help of the salespeople. Mrs. Neudorf prefers in-store purchasing because it gives her the undivided attention of the company representative and allows her to compare items with Clovis's existing merchandise. Each company representative visits Clovis Jewellers two or three times a year, usually in the spring and early fall.

Mr. Neudorf has arranged special payment terms with approximately 75 percent of his suppliers. The credit terms are usually 30/60 days, 30/60/90 days, 30/60/90/120 days, or even up to six months; most companies will give these terms free of any interest charges. Mr. Neudorf finds these terms necessary for cash flow management, as the majority of purchases are made during slow sales periods.

Mr. Neudorf maintains a tight level of quality control, inspecting each piece of jewellery before it is put on sale. Each item is checked for diamond or gemstone quality, quality of stone settings, and adequate stamping of gold quality. Items that do not meet the strict quality standards are returned to the supplier for exchange.

A purchasing budget is prepared by multiplying the target gross margin percentage by the budgeted sales figure. This total purchase figure is then spread out throughout the year according to monthly sales, with the majority of purchases made in the pre-Christmas season.

Inventory Control. No formal inventory control method is used at Clovis Jewellers. Mr. and Mrs. Neudorf rely on experience when it comes to controlling inventory levels. Visual inspections determine whether inventory levels are sufficient or need replenishing. No automatic reorder procedure is used; Mr. and Mrs. Neudorf believe automatic reordering would hurt rather than enhance sales because customers expect to find unique pieces of jewellery at Clovis.

Mr. Neudorf has insurance to cover fire, loss of merchandise stored in the safe, loss of customer goods stored in the safe, and business interruption (up to six months). Insurance to protect against theft of merchandise not stored in the safe is either not available or too expensive. All of the rings and diamond jewellery are placed in the safe after business hours; therefore, most of Clovis's inventory is insured in the event of a break-in. The business interruption insurance is related to inventory; a major loss or damage of inventory would not force Clovis Jewellers out of business, as the firm would continue to have a daily cash flow.

Accounting and Financial

Recording and Classifying. The daily and weekly recording and classifying done by the staff at Clovis Jewellers basically follows a one-write system, with the addition of certain journals and a daily cash summary. The one-write system, kept by Mr. Neudorf, is used to maintain all of the sundry (nonmerchandise) accounts as well as the company payroll. The nonmerchandise accounts are paid as they arise and therefore require almost daily attention; the payroll is calculated every two weeks.

A daily cash summary is prepared by Mr. Neudorf every weekday morning (Friday's and Saturday's are prepared on Monday). This cash summary includes a summary of the day's sales, both cash sales and charge sales; a summary of how the cash flow is distributed, including cash expenses and bank deposits; and a record of returned merchandise and cheques. The main purpose of this cash summary is to ensure that the cash transactions balance on a day-to-day basis.

Mr. Neudorf also keeps an accounts payable ledger, which he updates weekly. Proper managing of the accounts payable is important to Clovis Jewellers because it relies on trade credit to purchase all of its inventories. A journal of monthly purchases is kept to maintain control over the inventory and the merchandise purchases. Mrs. Neudorf is responsible for keeping this journal up to date; usually she adds all of the invoices to the journal at the end of the month, when a total can be calculated.

One final area in which recording is done on a day-to-day basis is the jewellery repair journal and record of ring sales. Clovis Jewellers has an extensive jewellery and watch repair department. The repair department is run by the sales staff and involves entering every repair job into a journal for easy reference. Because of the quick turnover of repair jobs (usually one to two days), they must be entered into the journal the same day they are received to prevent any bottlenecks in the system. Individual ring sales are also recorded in a book for quick reference as needed.

Budgeting. Five years ago, the budgeting process was almost nonexistent at Clovis Jewellers. Except for some very rough, off-the-top-of-the-head figures, no budgets were prepared. This has changed in the last few years, and although the budgetary process still needs improvement, it has taken a definite shape and form.

The process starts with a sales budget. This budget is prepared by looking at last year's sales and then updating them based on any special considerations for the upcoming year. The budget is prepared monthly and used to make regular comparisons with actual sales figures.

Once the sales budget is complete, a merchandise purchases budget is prepared based on the specific level of monthly sales. The purchases budget includes all shares of merchandise purchases, including the cost of repairs.

An expense budget is prepared by Mr. Neudorf. Again, previous years' expense totals are used. These expense totals are evaluated as being too high, too low, or correct over the past year and are then changed accordingly for the upcoming budgeted year. The budgeting of all the expense totals is very important, as it allows for better control of these expenses as they are incurred.

The final budget prepared is the cash flow project budget. This is done by combining the projected sales, merchandise payments, and expense budgets. This cash flow projection is very important for Clovis Jewellers, because the seasonal cash inflows it experiences often creates cash shortages; the cash flow analysis allows Mr. Neudorf to plan for these shortages.

Financial Statements. Clovis Jewellers has a complete set of financial statements prepared once a year by a certified general accounting firm (see Appendix 2 on pages 465–467). The statements are prepared after January 31 of each year, which Mr. Neudorf has chosen as the year-end date due to the low volume of business and low inventory count that occur at this time. All financial statements are prepared showing the previous year's figures for purposes of easy comparison.

The balance sheet is prepared in the traditional format, with assets on the left side of the statement and liabilities and equity on the right. Current assets constitute roughly 75 percent of the total assets; inventory is the largest and most important part of the current assets. Clovis Jewellers has a long-term loan payable, which makes up the largest part of the total liabilities. This loan contract is held with the Bank of Montreal and carries personal guarantees from both Mr. Neudorf and his business associate, Fred Meyer.

An income statement is prepared based on sales and expense figures supplied by Mr. Neudorf. This statement does not include a detailed list of the operating expenses. For this purpose, a detailed statement of operating expenses is prepared. This statement lists each expense totalled for the year and in alphabetical order.

A statement of changes in financial position is also prepared at year-end. This statement explains how funds were generated and used throughout the year. The purpose of this statement is to indicate any changes in the working capital of the business and explain how those changes occurred.

Planning

Long-Term Planning. Management at Clovis Jewellers appears to be typical of most small businesses in that a serious lack of any long-term planning exists. The only long-term planning that has occurred is the signing of a five-year lease. Although this means of planning is extremely informal by even a liberal definition, it indicates that some consideration has been given to the long-range plans of Clovis Jewellers.

Short-Term Planning. Mr. Neudorf engages in a number of forms of short-term planning. Among them are budgeting for the upcoming year, planning promotions, and cash flow planning. Budgets are prepared early in the fiscal year and extend to the end of the year. The budgets include a sales budget, a purchases budget, and an expense budget. The budgetary process is still in the early stages of development, but an increased awareness on the part of Mr. Neudorf ensures that it will be an effective form of short-term planning in the future.

Promotions are planned on an informal basis; no concrete goals or objectives are stated. Most of the promotions are planned based on the success of the previous year's promotions. If a promotion proved successful one year, it is automatically considered for the next year. This method produces mixed results, as some promotions are successful one year and quite unsuccessful the next.

One area of short-range planning that requires attention is the planning of future cash flows. Mr. Neudorf prepares a complete cash flow analysis for the upcoming year based on projected sales, merchandise purchases, and expenses. This cash flow analysis does not always prove accurate due to extraordinary items that arise in the course of the year, but at least it gives Mr. Neudorf a plan for goals for which to aim.

Appendix 1

Clovis Jewellers: Organizational Structure

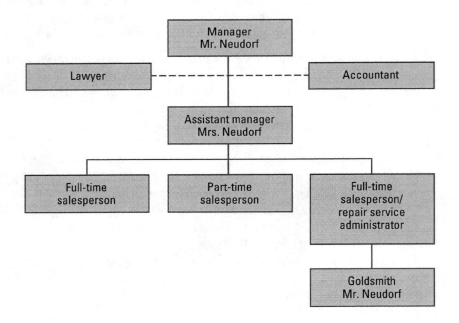

Appendix 2

Clovis Jewellers: Financial Statements

CLOVIS JEWELLERS (1978) LTD.
Balance Sheet
(Unaudited)
January 31, 2005

	2005	2004
Assets		
Current		
Cash	$ 24,886.15	$ 32,834.17
Accounts receivable (trade)	4,885.34	5,725.74
(shareholders)	18,186.40	18,462.84
Inventory	190,612.90	197,318.70
Prepaid expense	8,437.01	9,150.01
	247,007.80	263,491.46
Assets		
Investments	1,045.00	—
Fixed	10,853.69	13,566.69
Other		
Goodwill less amortization	56,672.20	59,228.20
Incorporation costs	—	373.54
Due from Neudorf holdings	15,448.95	15,448.95
	$ 331,027.64	$ 352,108.84
Liabilities		
Current:		
Accounts payable and accruals	$ 70,987.17	$ 92,214.96
Employee remittance payable	1,447.75	1,539.07
Corporation taxes payable	925.40	834.85
Current portion of long-term	11,316.00	8,000.00
	84,676.32	102,588.88
Long-Term	199,961.77	214,156.14
	284,638.09	316,745.02
Shareholders' Equity		
Share Capital	$ 100.00	$ 100.00
Retained Earnings	46,289.55	35,263.82
	46,389.55	35,363.82
	$ 331,027.64	$ 352,108.84

CLOVIS JEWELLERS (1978) LTD.
Statement of Income
(Unaudited)
Year Ended January 31, 2005

	2005	2004
Sales	$ 420,559.99	$ 472,035.50
Cost of Sales	218,332.01	261,016.36
Gross Margin	202,227.98	211,019.14
Selling Expenses	192,626.33	210,073.57
Operating Income	9,601.65	945.57
Other Income:		
Interest earned	350.48	213.63
Gain from sale of assets	—	1,133.00
Income before Taxes	9,952.13	2,292.20
Income taxes	925.40	834.85
Net Income	$ 9,026.73	$ 1,457.35

CLOVIS JEWELLERS (1978) LTD.
Statement of Operating Expenses
(Unaudited)
Year Ended January 31, 2005

	2005	2004
Operating Expense:		
Accounting	$ 761.20	$ 1,039.30
Advertising	11,024.93	33,250.03
Amortization	4,556.00	4,556.00
Auto expenses	1,794.77	3,146.33
Bank charges and interest	4,318.90	4,549.10
Canada Pension Plan	1,201.94	1,296.32
Donations	350.00	350.00
Depreciation	2,713.00	3,391.00
Employment insurance	2,492.46	2,539.19
Equipment rental	4,200.00	2,700.00
Interest	28,016.38	30,747.77
Insurance	3,047.00	3,079.41
Legal expenses	448.54	80.09
Memberships and dues	510.00	587.74
Postage and stationery	1,382.82	2,388.12
Rent	28,965.29	28,175.00

CLOVIS JEWELLERS (1978) LTD.
Statement of Operating Expenses (*continued*)
(Unaudited)
Year Ended January 31, 2005

Repairs and maintenance	432.41	464.59
Salaries	82,180.91	74,505.54
Security	711.39	681.25
Supplies	2,224.87	2,308.94
Taxes	2,603.75	3,144.88
Telephone	983.67	1,104.04
Travel and promotion	3,764.89	1,621.14
Utilities	3,818.71	4,092.59
Workers' compensation	122.50	245.00
Total expenses	$ 192,626.33	$ 210,073.57